Squeezing Desire Through a Sieve

Squeezing Desire
Through a Sieve

Micro-essays
on Judgement & Justice

M T C Cronin

PUNCHER & WATTMANN

First published in 2009, reprinted 2024.

Published by Puncher and Wattmann
PO Box 279
Waratah NSW 2998

http://www.puncherandwattmann.com

office@puncherandwattmann.com

NATIONAL
LIBRARY
OF AUSTRALIA

A catalogue record for this book is available from the National Library of Australia

Cronin, M T C
1963 -
Squeezing Desire Through a Sieve: Micro-Essays on Judgement & Justice

ISBN   9781921450129

Cover design by Matthew Holt

Printed by Lightning Source International

contents

iii
randomness & reason,
imagination & wickedness...

iv
blindness & appearance,
identity & disguise...

part vii
irresponsibility & purpose,
drifting & death...

This man is so little of a poet, so little spiritual,
that he would disgust even a solicitor.

Charles Baudelaire
'Squibs', *Intimate Journals*

i

instability & buoyancy,
undecidability & groundlessness…

the drowning man & the watcher
(or 'how to give hope')

In the smallest hour of the day, the hour so unnoticed that it was permitted to go on and on, a man, a formidable man, was walking along the riverbank. This is a lesson in seeing, in avoiding tripping over the actions of others, in attending first to the blackness in one's own soul, an attention for which there will never be enough time. Could the strolling man swim? He had long ago misplaced all his trophies. It can honestly be said that he was at a stage in his life when such things were of no regard to him. He is running through his mind the phrase 'the bit above the neck' which he had read in an article by the feminist legal academic, Ngaire Naffine, when indeed he saw that very thing. It was as if his thought had been hunted down in its abyss and dragged across what could not be seen of the day before being slapped onto the surface of the river which was now mightily disturbed by its appearance. Its solidity! Indeed, he thought, indeed, though it must be admitted that he did not really admit the reality to himself. He was, after all, *deep* in thought, and the head which gaped and bobbled on the water like a ball pushed this way and that by the salivary nose of an excited dog was simply that, a head. He didn't think about swimming or what the law might or might not expect him to do. He watched the head although judging on appearances he might have presumed a body. Certainly, the head was attached to a great thrashing thing that kept pushing a scream up into the mouth where it could escape and there, unlike most escapees, try to draw some attention to itself. The thinking man may have deduced that this was a matter of life and death but deep thought, like autopoiesis, seeks to remake our perceptions of the social world. A certain clearness of vision can be a stumbling block. Take the 'waking up in the morning' metaphor: our man had in fact arisen a brighter, bubblier character when several hours ago he'd bounced out of bed. This was the end result of many disappointments and vicissitudes of life which yesterday had come to a head (disregard the pun and the plausibility of premonition!) causing the man to consciously 'uplift' himself, a task requiring massive willpower but which also had the unexpected consequence of protecting him from any feelings he might have in the future. He had become more of a man of action, it could be put – but notably a man of his *own* action. This safeguard meant compassion was reduced to a minimum – like a small plan which could be folded and pocketed – while the immune system was strengthened promising longer life. An accompanying happiness operated to remove the uniqueness of the situation he presently found himself witness to. The circumstance now presented itself as something quite able to be presented. Something that had been there a long time and was simply still there. Concomitant with this, and providing the paradox necessary for all things natural, it appeared to *dis*appear as something that had never really been and was/is thus always nothing. 'It was less a case of dying off than of failing to be born'[1] so to speak, although this line was spoken in the context of smallpox. Still '[a] sentence is never not in a context. We are never not in a situation... A sentence that seems to need no interpretation is already the product of one.'[2] And so the man on the riverbank said 'He appears to be going under' and kept on walking. (What *was* seen becomes 'neither head nor neck',[3] unspoken, 'sliding between photographic fidelity and fantasy, between iconicity and arbitrariness', a 'curious affair of embodiment and fragmentation'?[4]) Kept on walking... And what does the law say about going to the aid of someone who is drowning? Where does the law stand on Samaritans and non-Samaritans? Under the Common Law one who sees another drowning is under no obligation to rescue that person. Talk about decontextualization! This is consistent with the general Common Law rule which requires a special legal relationship to be present before the Common Law imposes a duty. This special legal relationship can be contractual, such as employer-employee, biological, i.e., parent-child, or involuntary such as a tort-feasor's relationship with the victim. Safe if you walk away and don't get involved (for involvement contains a sting for the brave: if you do get involved you must follow the rules!). Further, it's possible to sail away from whole sinking ships full of drowning people with no greater consequences than bleeding-heart public gossip and a bit of letters-to-the-newspaper wrist slapping. (Even governments can do it and are well-advised never to get involved with what might drag them down.) JUDGMENT: The strolling man does not need to lift a finger, let alone jump into the soup. He is not 'in the wrong'. And so documents without errors are murderers of what comes after. 'We're groggy, but let the guilt go. / Feel the motions of tenderness / around you, the buoyancy.'[5] A certain Bishop, Most Revered and Founding Chair, is reminded of a story about a person walking alongside a river who sees someone drowning: 'The person jumps in, pulls the victim out, and begins artificial respiration. While this is going on, another person calls for help; the rescuer jumps into the water again and pulls the new victim out. This process repeats itself several times until the rescuer gets up and walks away from the scene. A bystander approaches and asks in surprise where he is going, to which, the rescuer replies: "I am going upstream to find out who's pushing all these people in and see if I can stop it!"'[6] Viva system! As for the unlucky fellow in the water: 'It was only when the last person had gone, had left me, that I had hope, such terrible hope…'

shutting your eyes & walking in circles
(lessons in parsing)

The prisoner came before the court. Is this a joke? The police brought him! These 'Lessons in Parsing' are learned from the poet, Rashid Husain, who has 'burned the rules of syntax', who has 'burned the chains of grammar' and who has 'converted to the struggle'.[7] You cannot be *brought* to justice, you must *come*. Arriving at justice is 'active'. An active verb. Consider Paul Celan's little man with the scales:

> He put his virtues and vices, his innocence and guilt, his good and bad qualities on the scales because he wanted certainty before judging himself. But piled this way, the scales balanced.

As he wanted to know at any price, he shut his eyes and walked in circles around the scales, now clockwise, now counterclockwise, until he no longer knew which of the pans held which load. Then he blindly put on one of them his decision to judge himself.

Sure enough, when he opened his eyes again, one arm had gone down. But there was no way of knowing which: the scale of guilt or the scale of innocence.

This made him furious. He refused to see the advantage of the situation and sentenced himself — without, however, being able to shake off the feeling that he might be doing himself an injustice.'[8]

It seems you can even *bring* yourself. Even then there is no justice. But what might you know from the desire to know? From the desire to judge yourself? Rumi says: 'This we have now is not imagination. This is not grief or joy. Not a judging state, or an elation, or a sadness. Those come and go.'[9] There is wisdom in taking all the time in the world getting where you're going. 'The longer I withheld conclusion, the more I saw.'[10] 'So the sea-journey goes on, and who knows where!'[11] You do not know yourself until you know *what* are your imperfections. (The saint knows herself by her unsaintliness.) Until you know *what* your imperfections are. Study them and describe them fully from the point of view of classification, inflexion, and syntax. Then go somewhere else. (The sin is the little goodbye that doesn't want to depart.) You decide where. You might even arrive without them. 'We're groggy, but let the guilt go. Feel the motions of tenderness around you, the buoyancy.'[12] You might even come to where you are. Say 'Hello' to the unspeakable.

contrary to all regulations ~ rilke, the child

What might our juvenile justice system have done with Rilke, the child: 'At first I saw the actual park, away beyond the wide sandy foreground: first the grounds, which were reserved for the officers, in which, contrary to all regulations, I sometimes lost myself....'[13] Someone else equals a line. A regulation equals a line. 'Other people are the point of origin of a child's entry into the material/physical environment both in providing or inhibiting access to that environment – in making it – and in fostering entry into the language with which children learn to name.'[14] A five year old told me that it is by being naughty that you learn things. A child can be quite happy being naughty. I have wondered if only happy children are innocent. Regardless, Rilke knew that the aim was to lose the self. '[D]escent attaches itself to the body' states Foucault in his examination of Nietzsche's *Herkunft*, ('the ancient affiliation to a group, sustained by the bonds of blood, tradition, or social class').[15] The writers of the laws forbidding the little Rilke to set foot amongst the trees wrote those laws in Rilke's body – in his brain – so that the big Rilke would write:

> He went up under the gray leaves
> all gray and dissolved in olive country
> and laid his forehead full of dust
> deep in the dustiness of burning hands.
>
> ...
>
> For angels don't come to the prayers of such men,
> and nights don't grow large around them.
> The self-losing are let go by everything,
> and they are abandoned by their fathers
> and locked out of their mothers' wombs.[16]

And they are more than over the line – they are beyond the law. Shame is true but only for the shamer. Remorse is true. So is what is seen when justice is no longer a consideration because it should never be that. What did the child Rilke see in the park? He saw that he had a wax hand. He felt his heart pause. He understood hope and its groundlessness. He followed the hollow through himself and arrived sitting beside himself.

> That's how it is for a snake with two heads. First the two heads have to decide they're both hungry at the same time, and then they have to agree to pursue the same prey. Then they might fight over which head gets to swallow the prey. To make it even more complicated, since snakes operate a good deal by smell, if one head catches the scent of prey on the other's head, it will attack and try to swallow its second head.
>
> "They also have a great deal of difficulty deciding which direction to go, and if they had to respond to an attack quickly they would just not be capable of it," …[17]

But children are smart. Rilke edged away from himself so that he wasn't touching because '[i]f the two heads are very close together it's going to be much more difficult for them; with more separation, they can act a little more independently'.[18] The two little Rilke's could now compare what each had brought to where the other was:

> …I glide,
> Losing myself, out of my own hand,
> without hope of conquering
> what comes to me, as if out of your side,
> grave and stark and undeterred.
>
> … back then: O how complete I was,
> nothing calling, nothing that divulged me;[19]

Now *Things*. '...cups, spoons, chairs, trees, and flowers – ... the simplest and surest things that every adult knows. They are *there* to be known...'[20] 'The child must grow used to things, it must accept them; each thing has its pride.'[21] Outside the park it is time for tea. When Rilke the child left the park he was already punished. He had walked the hall of all that was forgotten and was able to leave himself. Emerging though he suddenly knew 'how grateful things are normally for tenderness, how such treatment breathes new life into them, indeed how (provided they are loved) even the roughest usage affects them like a devouring caress which admittedly makes them droop but also seems to endow them with a firmness of spirit which possesses them all the more strongly as their body yields...'[22] He now had to live his life. At the edge of childhood. Infused with the breath of others. To inexhaustibly live 'wholly and intimately integrated into human life'.[23] The name he gave to his experience was of a body which 'became indescribably touching to him and of no other use than that he might be present in it, purely and cautiously, exactly like a ghost, already living elsewhere, that sadly enters what has already been gently laid aside, in order to belong once more, though even absentmindedly, to a world once felt to be so indispensable.'[24] Or, as a three year old child said to me when I asked her what a ghost was like: 'I can't say because it makes me feel like a ghost. Please can I not explain a ghost.' Rilke disappeared illegally into that park at the end of his story – 'it matters a great deal how stories are framed'.[25] He began the same story with: 'I repeat: I find it quite comprehensible that those who have to depend entirely upon themselves, upon their own life's usefulness and bearableness, should feel a certain relief, if there is induced in them a spiritual nausea which enables them to rid themselves piece-wise of the misunderstandings and indigestible experiences of their childhood. But I? Am I not, indeed, born to form angels, things, animals, if need be, monsters, precisely in connection with such experiences, which were beyond experiencing, were too big, too premature, too horrible?'[26] What kind of decision – what answer – could ever provide justice for such a child, man, story as this?

where the judge is human
(*under the guise of an abhorrent buffoonery*[27])
leading into a conclusion of how history might judge
a spot on a suit

'Certainly, someone who decides the law instead of being its addressee cannot be a judge but is necessarily a criminal.'[28]

Or elegantly put, by someone, the judge is a 'civilized bull'.[29]

Once, on a literature festival panel about writing and drugs, I alluded to a 'world' or 'space' without judgement. A well-known, very middle-aged, widely-published and highly accomplished poet who autobiographically took lots of drugs in his youth (not sure about the years that followed) snorted and targeted me with the impossibility, indeed the ridiculousness, of such an idea. 'He that is without sin among you, let him cast the first stone'[30] I might have said, though this itself may have constituted some sort of judgement and anyhow, I was soon caught up in a silly argument with another poet in the audience concerning whether or not Rumi was being metaphorical with his use of the work 'drunk'. I am all for there having been some wine around at the time. Now Michaux, had he been present, would have done a better job and I can hear him reciting one of his travels:

> Even in the law courts they have never succeeded in maintaining a really balanced frame of mind.
>
> The Presiding Justice, about to judge a criminal loses his nerve: "I don't quite take it in," he says. "Let's suppose I am the criminal!" He asks for a knife, reenacts the murder, gets worried, leaves, returns, flees, gets arrested by the police, and

not infrequently the defendant uses the occasion to take to his heels, sometimes in the Presiding Justice's clothing.

For the latter plays his part in earnest, and removes his judicial robes. "I am just a simple criminal," he says, and the police thrash him soundly, and these lay on the others' skins so effectively that nobody really knows who is involved or what is the matter; the overzealous magistrate is stoned by the crowd for the horrible murder which he confesses and shamelessly reenacts. The witnesses, naturally well satisfied to see everything clearing up, solemnly swear that he is the one they saw break into the house where the crime was committed, and they demand immediate execution.

Another time the prisoner affirms: "Your honor, I hardly squeezed at all, see, only like this." Meanwhile he has clenched his hands around the neck of the Presiding Justice, who pulls away half-dead and incapable of pronouncing judgment. But the crowd, losing their patience at watching this spectacle which they haven't understood, demand that the pair of them – these damned wranglers – be sent to prison for years. The lawyers who have made everything complicated are thrown out the door, and the court empties in a thunderclap.'[31]

Problem is, these are the Hivinizikis and they may not even be human. (Michaux doesn't say and why should he? He has his experiments and he doesn't want to skew the results.) What happens where the judge is human? There might be humility but it doesn't reach the level of nakedness. There might be honesty but it would hardly amount to an admittance of guilt. There might be criminality and murderous intent but the judge would normally just sit there and pretend not to kill anyone. Even madness would be denied by the occasion. And everyone – from the accused to the police to the lawyers to the witnesses to the jury if there is one to those in the public gallery – goes along, floats along in this bubble of good sense and firm counsel because to do otherwise could result in some collective collapse and rebirth in an unknown form.

[May we go off on a tangent here?: Personally I would question the 'sense' of any activity which has at its heart the requirement that something be *proven*. But is prose – say, as opposed to poetry – one such activity? Take this little essay for example. I always get the secret suspicion when writing prose – any prose – that I am going to be judged. Judged both as a writer and for what and how I say it. (Not to mention judged on the *both* that is inseparable in that very word.) *Who* are you really to be saying this? No such fear attends my writing of poetry. Could this be because during prose I have something to prove? And why? Is it a matter of consequence? On the one hand we might go to Fernando Pessoa who in his disquiet claims that 'All art is contained in prose' and that poetry, like music, is subject to laws, *limited* by laws – rhythmic, decorous and of constraint, 'automatic precepts that oppress and punish. In prose we speak freely.'[32] Seems paradoxical. That in poetry I feel free when I am bound by discipline. In prose I am free and fearful. But perhaps this is it. At our most free we have most to lose. More rides on freedom. But only in a world where what is not free exists. If we were truly and purely free we would need neither art or judgement. We would become different kinds of humans. Art exists to celebrate what is 'despite imperfection'. It is to remind ourselves of why, and for what, judgement is still passed on us. Free, there is no need. It is possible that what we do now for art might still exist in this world but it would have a name like feeding or sleeping and there would be no debates about its relevance or necessity. In addition, it would not be losable.]

Anyhow, following the straight line of prose back to civilization and the judge in the court. What if the players refused to play the game and set upon each other with their imaginations? The phoenix arising may have no need or desire to judge. Order sees this as chaos when in reality it might be a release from the mediocrity of standards. This does not necessarily entail disinterest. It might do away with preference. Love is there in abundance. The face has simultaneously every look on it. 'Even when a full understanding is attained, however, it waxes and wanes…'[33] One might rise as prosecutor to persuasively address the bench and find oneself impassive in the dock receiving the sentence of one's own death with the 'unpanicky response of a pig to a storm'.[34] One might in chains shuffle into the court to find the King's new mistress has suggested a National Day of Picnic and you are free to go, basket and all! Or the chamber may be empty and a nice large space for you to perform cartwheels whilst whistling. What if the place is simply unrecognizable? 'Consider the strangeness a traveler experiences in a country and culture where she has to suspend judgments about the identity and nature of all manner of things from simple artifacts, to flora and fauna, to customs and cultural phenomona.'[35] Knowing your fellows, would you like them to judge you? If a judge was really familiar with your innermost thoughts, your complete history, how far do you think you'd get? If you knew the judge was 'only human' would you trust them to do you justice? But do you know what happens to those who refuse to judge (you don't really have much of a choice about being judged)? They become the subject of much amusement and on an evolutionary level humour is connected directly to suffering – the pain of being wrong according to one Mr Dorrell. 'To sum it up in a slogan: we do not enjoy being presented with evidence that shows we might be wrong, but we do enjoy being presented with evidence that shows that we really, really are wrong.'[36] Laugh! All jokes are sick. Soon they'll be kicking and crucifying you. (Do you think the name of this case is funny: *R v Bow Street Magistrate; Ex Parte Pinochet (2)*?) Not to mention sniggering that you're an idealist because you've tossed into the conversation a rather nice idea: not a heart 'as efficient as a bull's / and as desperate / for the earth's treasures'[37] but

The confused memory / Of crimes in common.

See us now, thrown face to face
So as to comprehend.[38]

To judge is to claim familiarity with another. To suspend judgment is to know oneself and 'To know oneself is to make a mistake'.[39]

> The man of just sensibility and proper reason, if he finds himself concerned with the evil and injustice in the world, naturally seeks to correct them, first that which appears closest to him; and he will find it in his own being. This task will take him his entire life.[40]

Mistakes, of course, are what make us laugh and it's from a good mistake that we learn. Why talk about the judge as a civilized bull? 'Aristotle says that metaphor causes the mind to experience itself in the act of making a mistake.'[41] 'Metaphors teach the mind to enjoy error and to learn from the juxtaposition of *what is* and *what is not* the case.'[42] The judge therefore can hardly undertake the task he is named for — deciding the case — if he is going to be perceived to be in any way reasonable. He must examine himself, announce his disguise and set about reducing the courtroom to an uncontrollable hysteria. Anything less is sure to trigger an unstoppable history of 'naming, claiming and blaming'.[43]

> I bought a suit around the last of May. I wore the suit once and sent it to the cleaners. When the suit came back, there was a spot on it. The man at the cleaners told me that there was a defect in the material. I took the suit home and told my wife what the cleaner has said. We agreed that I should take it back again to the cleaners the next day. He agreed to reclean the suit. When it came back a second time no different from the first,

26

the cleaner offered to send it away to have the fabric analyzed. He promised to refund my money if the analysis proved that he was at fault. He got my suit back two weeks later with a report saying that he wasn't at fault but I don't agree.[44]

In conclusion, at that literature and drugs panel (a brief recount of which served as my introduction), there was no-one in a suit. Regardless, I was judged and to this day obviously bear the blemish. This is it. This little bruise of an essay. I can only hope that it in turn won't be taken for a judgment or the pain and misunderstanding could go on and on. History is, of course, the classic and hopeless stalemate.

ENDNOTES

1. A Sutherland in Henry Reynolds, *Dispossession – Black Australians and White Invaders*, Allen & Unwin, St Leonard's, 1989, p11 (speaking of smallpox).

2. Stanley Fish, 'Normal Circumstances, Literal Language, Direct Speech Acts, the Ordinary, the Everyday, the Obvious, What Goes Without Saying, and Other Special Cases' in *Is There a Text in This Class?*, Cambridge, Massachusetts, 1980, p284.

3. Michael Taussig, *Mimesis and Alterity, A Particular History of the Senses,* Routledge, New York, London, 1993, p17.

4. *Ibid.*

5. Jelaluddin Rumi, 'Buoyancy', *The Essential Rumi,* (versions by Coleman Barks), HarperCollins, San Francisco, 1995, p105.

6. Saint John's Abbey and University Collegeville, Minnesota 56321 USA, Web - www.csbsju.edu/isti email – isti@csbsju.edu, Bishop John Kinney welcomes ISTI conference participants: the most reverend John F Kinney is the Roman Catholic Bishop of Saint Cloud Diocese, Minnesota, and founding chair of the United States National Catholic Conference of Bishops' (nccb) committee on clergy sexual abuse. His welcoming address to the participants of the isti national conference in collegeville on 13, 14, 15 June, is printed in its entirety.

7. Rashid Husain, 'Lessons in Parsing', from Salma Khadra Jayyusi, ed., *Modern Arabic Poetry, An Anthology,* Columbia University Press, New York, 1987, p269.

8. Paul Celan, from 'Backlight', *Collected Prose*, (translated by Rosmarie Waldrop), Carcanet, Manchester, 1986, pp13-14.

9. Jelaluddin Rumi, 'This We Have Now', *op cit*, p261.

10. Louise Glück, 'Education of the Poet', *Proofs & Theories: Essays on Poetry,* The Ecco Press, New Jersey, 1994, pp12-13.

11. Rumi, 'Buoyancy, *op cit*, p105.

12. Rumi, 'This We Have Now', *op cit*, p105.

13. Rainer Maria Rilke, 'Memory', *Rodin and Other Prose Pieces,* Quartet Books Limited, London, 1986, p118.

14. Lorraine Code, *Rhetorical Spaces, Essays on Gendered Locations,* Routledge, New York, 1995, p45.

15. Michel Foucault, 'Nietzsche, Genealogy, History', from Paul Rabinow, ed., *The Foucault Reader,* Peregrine Books, Penguin Books, Harmondsworth, Middlesex, England, 1986 (1984), pp80-81.

16. Rainer Maria Rilke, 'The Olive Garden', *New Poems [1907]*, (A Bilingual Edition translated by Edward Snow), North Point Press, Farrar Straus and Giroux, New York, 1995 (1984), pp40-41.

17. Hillary Mayell, 'Life is Confusing for Two-Headed Snakes', www.nationalgeographic.com.

18. *Ibid.*

19. Rainer Maria Rilke, 'Woman in Love', *The Book of Images* (Bilingual Edition translated by Edward Snow, Newly Revised), North Point Press, Farrar. Straus and Giroux, New York, 1994 (1991), p23.

20. Lorraine Code, *op cit*, p45.

21. Rainer Maria Rilke, 'Dolls: On the Wax Dolls of Lotte Pritzel' from Heinrich Von Kleist, Charles Baudelaire, Rainer Maria Rilke, *Essays on Dolls,* (translated by Idris Parry and Paul Keegan), Syrens, Penguin Books, London, 1994, p34. Rilke's essay first published 1913/14.

22. *Ibid*, p29.

23. *Ibid.*

24. Rainer Maria Rilke, 'An Experience', *Rodin and Other Prose Pieces*, *op cit*, p111.

25. Kim Lane Scheppele, 'Foreward: Telling Stories', Vol.87, *Michigan Law Review,* 1989, pp2073-2098, p2085.

26. Rainer Maria Rilke, 'Memory', *Rodin and Other Prose Pieces*, *op cit*, p116.

27. David Rousset's description quoted by Jean-Francois Lyotard, *The Differend; Phrases in Dispute,* (translation by Georges Van Den Abbeele), University of Minnesota Press, Minneapolis, 1988 (1983), p107.

28. Jean-Francois Lyotard, *op cit*, p107.

29. Somebody somewhere judged judges to be 'civilized bulls'.

30. John 8:7.

31. Henri Michaux, *Selected Writings, The Space Within,* (translated by Richard Ellman), New Directions, New York, 1968, pp173, 175.

32. Fernando Pessoa, *The Book of Disquiet, Composed by Bernardo Soares, Assistant Bookkeeper in the City of Lisbon,* (translated by Alfred Mac Adam), Exact Change, Boston, 1998, p267.

33. Raymond Gaita, *A Common Humanity, Thinking About Love & Truth & Justice,* Text Publishing, Melbourne, Australia, 1999, p43.

34. Felipe Fernandez-Armesto, *Truth, A History and a Guide for the Perplexed,* Black Swan, London, 1998 (1997), p123.

35. Lorraine Code, *What Can She Know? Feminist Theory and the Construction of Knowledge,* Cornell University Press, Ithaca and London, 1991, p39.

36. Philip Dorrell, *What is Humour,* 1999, http://www.1729.com/index.html.

37. Robert Adamson, 'The home, the spare room', *Mulberry Leaves, New & Selected Poems 1970-2001,* Paper Bark Press, Sydney, 2001, pp156-7. Poem originally from *The Law at Heart's Desire.*

38. Guillevic, *Carnac,* Bloodaxe Contemporary French Poets: 9, (translated by John Montague, Introduction by Stephen Romer), Bloodaxe Books, Newcastle upon Tyne, 1999 (1961), p133.

39. Fernando Pessoa, *op cit*, p264.

40. *Ibid*, p265.

41. Anne Carson, 'Essay on What I Think About Most', *Men in the Off Hours*, Alfred A Knopf, New York, 2000, p30.

42. *Ibid*, p31.

43. From the title of the article: William Felstiner, Richard Abel and Austin Sarat, 'The emergence and transformation of disputes: Naming, blaming, claiming…', *Law and Society Review*, Vol 15, 1980-81.

44. John M Conley and William M O'Barr, *Just Words: Law, Language and Power*, The University of Chicago Press, Chicago and London, 1998, p85.

ii

usefulness & uselessness,
conversation & contingency...

a little bit of equipollence goes a long way
or does it?

Equipollence is the term used by Sextus Empiricus to express the view that there are arguments of equal strength on all sides of any question and that therefore we should suspend judgement on every question that can be raised.[1]

To take an example: The appeal book shall be divided into 3 sections:

1. The formal section bound in a red cover – the Red Book
2. The transcript section bound in a black or grey cover – the Black Book
3. The document section bound in a blue cover – the Blue Book

Why is the Red Book, red; the Blue Book, blue; yet the Black Book can be black or grey? Is grey *like* black, while red is red and blue is blue? Is colour debatable? Is colour deceitful (as in 'being coloured')? If colour is a sensation can it ever be actual? Plausible? Feigned?

Not to mention the queries that might arise from the government brochure which states:

> [t]he manual dexterity of the Oriental female is famous the world over. Her hands are small, and she works fast with extreme care...[2]

A moot point?

Or you might ask: Does anyone ever think of a sausage without thinking of another?

There is no end to this sort of thing.

So what is law's answer? Sausage-justice?[3]

Now *sausage* is a funny word.

Or is it?

the trivial nature of confession
(or 'i woke up to find i was a murderer')

The best advice you will ever receive is 'DO NOT CONFESS!'

Your confession is absolutely useless to anyone but yourself and for yourself it is a trivialization. (More about the latter later.) Legal practice, in the meantime, thrives on narrative and prizes confession as part of the story. (It doesn't, however, use the word *narrative* or the word *story*. (Though sometimes the second is heard around the traps – derogatory naturally – as in, 'Well, that's *his* story!)) 'We want the truth' say the enforcers of the law. (Inner certainties versus outer certitude?) 'The truth' say the upholders of the law. Aha, the truth! (The truth as it is constantly being alleged.) (What about the denial of denial (of justice)?) But not just the truth. Only the truth if you tell it to us. In your own words. (Words being things of inestimable value.) And so it is possible that you might say... well, anything!

>...he was trembling when he was found
>...I have brought 500 years of killing to a halt
>...the sex was just padding

How weak is possibility's shell. How intimate justice? How many lies can add up to the truth. Though making legal truth can be both easier or harder to conjure than any other kind. For as far as the law is concerned it is all about getting away with it – or not! Sounds simple. It's not. You might want to tell the truth only to find your evidence is inadmissible. You may not wish to hide what you are not asked yet you are prohibited from speaking unless questioned. It may be that the law allows you to reply but only wants half of your answer. After all, '[w]e don't get closer to "the truth" by describing "more"'.[4] There is a certain dullness to all this that I would advise you not to become a part of.

If you really want to confess, the desire evinces another desire — that you wish to take yourself seriously — and its concomitant need, that having taken yourself too seriously you must now lighten the load by spilling the beans. (Talking, babbling, loosening the lips. Gossip, chatter, runaway tongue.) Be honest. This trivializes your position. (After all, how can anything about you be a lie?) Be honest. (Unburdening oneself is exactly that!) Be honest. Confession is never what it is cracked up to be. (Those who confess inevitably wind up confessing someone else along with them.) Tell me, why do you feel the need?

Would you like to be let into a secret? You cannot be saved though you may relinquish any reasons for which you might need saving.

the tort of criminal conversation
& suffering in the right ear

Having sex with the plaintiff's wife, certain issues are clear: 'Following the accident Mrs Smith lost interest in sex and commenced suffering in her right ear.' Her husband, Mr Smith, slept on the right side of the bed. He has maintained she heard nothing. Yet we have admitted into evidence as Exhibit A a poem allegedly written by him and published last year in the left-wing newspaper, *Green Left*.

EXHIBIT A:

MILLIONS OF SECRETS — APRIL 4

Last year the Government
Created 6.8 million secrets
Roughly the same number
As the previous year
But that doesn't take into account
The effects of the war
Said an annual report
Issued yesterday

I promised I would never tell
But they cut off
A man's balls in front of me
I couldn't stop talking

The President wrote a letter
Accompanying the report
To praise the Government
For keeping secrets during the war
While providing for
An informed public

When my wife whispers
In my ear
In my bed
My cock dies
And I sweat
But we keep our secrets

Counsel for the plaintiff would probably like to maintain that it is *his* – the plaintiff's – and not *her* – the plaintiff's wife's, ear that is in issue here. After all, in the poem he has her do the whispering into his ear. However, this is what they call in the business a red herring although the poem would suggest it to be a kind of rude hearing. He does say elsewhere in the poem that he couldn't stop talking and as far as this court is concerned that amounts to a confession, albeit lyrical. Thus, I don't think we need to hear from Counsel at all. Secrets were obviously not kept – despite poetic protests to the contrary – (take note of the term 'our secrets' in stanza four). We can, in this most obvious of cases, dispense with the hearing and proceed directly to sentence. But first, a brief judicial homily.

HOMILY:

Torture exists for a reason. To take heed of it. 'If you are not a Vietcong, we will beat you until you admit you are; and if you admit you are, we will beat you until you no longer dare to be one.'[5] The irrelevance is really quite secret. Torture, even when, as in this case, once-removed, 'is the inversion of the trial, a reversal of cause and effect. While the one studies evidence that may lead to punishment, the other uses punishment to generate the evidence.'[6] 'If they are not guilty, beat them until they are'.[7] Both are a study in importance. The secret is really quite irrelevant. Justice is only a whisper in the ear. What the interrogator and the judge hear is part of their strategy. The 'questioning' and the 'Hearing' make judgement possible. It may be that judgement entails (an)other but 'Power is cautious. It covers itself. It bases itself in another's pain and prevents all recognition that there is "another" by looped circles that ensure its own solipsism.'[8]

SENTENCE:

The plaintiff and his wife are found guilty of the presumption of believing themselves snakes simultaneously swallowing each other's tails. As well they seem to be talking under the misconception that what they hear is not contingent upon what they say. They are hereby sentenced to twin beds (each out of hearing of the other).

learning how to lift:
sensitivity, prudence & the 65 kilogram desk

Evidence was also given by Mr. Ross Anthony Power, a man who has been in the business of selling secondhand government desks, and perforce of lifting and moving desks, for over 20 years. He is unusually sensitive to the dangers involved in the lifting of furniture, possibly because he was once the foreman in charge of furniture removals for the Commonwealth of Australia in the Australian Capital Territory. He is a trained kinetic lifting trainer, that is, he has been taught how to teach people how to lift. His staff of 26 have all had at least one week of training in lifting. He sets an example of prudence and of safety consciousness that is perhaps higher than what might be expected to be matched by the ordinary employer. Indeed, I find it hard to see how a whole week could be spent in learning how to lift. But the very familiarity of the act of lifting should put the reasonable employer on notice of the risk involved in leaving an employee like the plaintiff to try to cope without assistance in the repeated movement of awkward and heavy objects such as the desk in question. I do not think that such an employer needs to send the employee for training in lifting or even to give instruction in lifting. Furthermore, it is by no means clear what the plaintiff, properly instructed, could have done in the circumstances except to do what she did. Even Dr Adams concedes that she was using the only technique possible for a person performing that type of task unaided. Supervision likewise could have been of no practical benefit in the circumstances unless it became in effect either the prohibition of carrying out the task or the actual rendering of manual assistance.[9]

It seems kind of quaint, doesn't it, to consider lifting in such a serious manner? It makes us smile to ourselves, reading this extract. But why? Consider the judge's words: *Indeed, I find it hard to see how a whole week could be spent in learning how to lift.* Would the coach of an Olympic weight-lifter find it hard to see? What about those in the Santa Barbara County

Fire Department who train their Community Emergency Response Team in the lifting of heavy objects? Perhaps this judge has never had to lift heavy objects or has forgotten the few times he did. But really, what is he creating here with his words? Does his skepticism create a space in which we imagine the learning of lifting to be reasonably accomplished in say five days, or no, maybe seventy-two hours, or then again, in perhaps a mere half-day of intensive instruction? Are there natural lifters? Those who can safely have a piano off the ground in no time at all? Are there some who can't lift to save themselves. Those who even after a degree in lifting have no idea really how to hoist a box of bananas?

Regardless, I am curious as to whether the judge laboured over the writing of this judgment.

> I write, erase, rewrite,
> erase again, and then
> a poppy blooms. [10]

Does judging, and the articulation of the judgment – pen to paper, fingertips to the keyboard – come as naturally as lifting a finger to a nose? What's assumed here I suppose, both in the examination of the lifting and in the judgement of the judgment, are the matters of wellness and capability. How well, after all, was the woman able to move the desk? Women are often required – expected – to pass the lifting buck if there's a man around. This would seem to hold even where the man is smaller and weaker than the woman. Judges too are excused for writing tedious and obfuscating judgments on the grounds that they are lawyers and not poets. However, they are often men and so would seem to have something in common with the class that is held to be naturally capable of lifting. Further, some of the best judgments ever written are intensely poetic and far more than 'just words': 'Words are useless by themselves; what the words can do is the very reverse of useless.' [11] Which is just as well because in one particular prison 'a useless word is punishable',[12] something which makes me wonder why useless words spoken or written anywhere aren't immediately met with punishment. Such would demand prudence and sensibility to precede any utterance at all and would no doubt gradually bring about a general situation whereby, like the ideal scenario concerning the movement of a 65kg desk, there would either be a prohibition of carrying out the task or the actual rendering of manual assistance by someone who knew better. Possibly a poet.

ENDNOTES

1. Sextus – a Greek Skeptic philosopher of the third century A.D. – also denies that he is saying anything dogmatically: 'he is just stating how he feels at given moments. He hopes that dogmatists sick with a disease, rashness, will be cured and led to tranquility no matter how good or bad the Skeptical arguments might be.' See Robert Audi, General Editor, *The Cambridge Dictionary of Philosophy,* Second Edition, Cambridge University Press, Cambridge, 1999, p278 and pp838-9.

2. Malaysian Government brochure.

3. See Patricia Williams, *The Alchemy of Race and Rights: Diary of a Law Professor,* Harvard University Press, Harvard, 1991, pp107-8, where Williams describes the law-making process as a 'sausage-making machine'.

4. Lief Carter, 'Book Review of Toward a New Common Sense: Law, Science and Politics in the Paradigmatic Transition by Boaventura de Sousa Santos, Routledge, New York and London, 1995' in *The Law and Politics Book Review,* Vol.6, No.10, October, 1996, pp157-161 (electronic periodical).

5. Elaine Scarry, *The Body in Pain ~ The Making and Unmaking of the World,* Oxford University Press, New York, Oxford, 1985, pp41-42.

6. *Ibid*, p41.

7. *Ibid*.

8. *Ibid*, p59.

9. Court case – lost to history.

10. Hokushi, from *Japanese Death Poems, Written by Zen Monks and Haiku Poets on the Verge of Death,* (compiled and with an introduction by Yoel Hoffman), Tuttle Publishing, Boston; Rutland, Vermont; Tokyo, 1986, p190.

11. Idries Shah, 'Reactions', *Thinkers of the East, Studies in Experientialism,* The Octagon Press, London, 2002, p73.

12. Michel Foucault, speaking of the prison Mettray from Jean Genet's *The Miracle of the Rose* in 'The Carceral', Paul Rabinow, ed., *The Foucault Reader,* Peregrine Books, Penguin Books, Harmondsworth, Middlesex, England, 1986 (1984), p235.

iii

randomness & reason,
imagination & wickedness...

opal ruby pearl barlow ~ an act of caprice

This case[1] goes back quite a number of years. Tried in 1949 after an incident which allegedly occurred in 1946 in a suburban hotel. A hotel by the beach in fact where Opal Ruby Pearl Barlow was a barmaid. She was referred to by a 'senior female employee who witnessed it' [the incident], as 'You wicked girl', so we might presume that she was youngish. Wicked? Perhaps. Apparently what she did – 'the act' – 'was dictated by a desire purely personal to the barmaid' and the person she did it to – the plaintiff, Mr Flew – was 'otherwise damnified' by her act. Heady stuff! In cross-examination this Mr Flew, who should always be referred to as 'the plaintiff', said that 'he remembered knocking over a glass of beer, that is was quite likely that he called the barmaid foul names [quite unnecessary when she already had such pretty ones](which reflected upon her chastity and parentage), but he did not remember striking her.' Numerous other descriptions were found for the barmaid's act including that it was capricious, an irresponsible urge and in 'truth' 'an act of passion and resentment done neither in furtherance of the master's interests nor under his express or implied authority nor as an incident to or in consequence of anything the barmaid was employed to do. It was a spontaneous act of retributive justice.' The trial court found both her and her employers liable. On appeal her act was seen as 'personal' and thus, though the decision against her should stand, her employers were entitled as a matter of law to a verdict. Reprieve! Our barmaid slips out of the building under the wing of her masters. But not for long. On further appeal by our Mr Flew her employers were again victorious but Opal Ruby Pearl was not. She must stand alone. Presumably as she did behind that bar. And what of her 'retributive justice'? We see from this case that justice may be reprehensible. Perhaps especially when meted out by a young woman of whom there was 'no evidence that she had any further authority than that of a barmaid'. And what do barmaids do? They serve.

POSTSCRIPT: In another case, *Petterson v Royal Oak Hotel Ltd*[2], it was found as a fact that when the bar*man* committed the act complained of he was carrying out the duty of keeping order.

nietzsche ~
his madness, his germanness, his maleness[3]

'If man really felt, there would be no civilization.'[4]

We are all, at heart, the peasant who hopes his neighbour's cow dies. We move all the way from 'what's mine is mine and yours, yours' to 'what's mine is yours' to 'if I can't have it neither will you' in the blink of an eye. We say horrible things about Nietzsche. We cannot spell his name without looking at it. Pronunciation springs from influence. We confuse our feelings with what we want. 'One of the subtlest ways of deceiving, for as long as possible at any rate, and of successfully posing as more stupid than one is – which in everyday life is often as desirable as an umbrella – is called *enthusiasm*: plus what belongs with it, for example virtue.'[5] What dance is reasonable? What defence necessary? We know love by how we fall short. The rules are to organize this chaos.

is heaven boring? what about justice?
chicken little shouts *"fiat justitia, ruat caelum"*
at a woman in a parachute

A gentleman by the name of Mark Ritter maintains that '[s]pending timelessness as a willing servant of the Most High can be nothing less' than 'the ultimate in growth, development, understanding, excitement, and fulfillment – Life as it was always meant to be.'[6] Further, Mr Ritter is a fact man:

> In our attempt to find out the truth about anything we might follow the advice of Dragnet's Sargent [sic] Joe Friday. "Just the facts, please," he would demand weekly. He was not concerned for rumor or hearsay or innuendo – he needed the facts to crack a case.
>
> So it is with inspecting Christianity. There are a lot of half-truths and fiction out there passing as truths and fact regarding the church founded by Jesus of Nazareth. Many people are rejecting Jesus based on these myths and misconceptions.

No. 9 on the myths and misconceptions list is the belief – I am unsure how widely held – that Heaven will be boring. Ritter appeals to our imagination:

> Picture this: The Almighty Creator of all the Universe, the Designer and Organizer of everything from the smallest subatomic particle to the most majestic of galaxies, the Giver of Life itself, the One who knows the heart and mind of every creature, the One Who can create from absolute nothing or annihilate at will, looks around Heaven and says with dismay, "Great! And I thought they would be happy – but just look at them! They're all bored stiff! Now what do I do???" It's hard

48

to fathom, after only a moment's reflection, that the Almighty Living God has an eternity of boredom awaiting us.

You might wonder. As you might wonder at the fact of God and the fact of Heaven and at the dizzying task of undertaking an inspection of Christianity. At least God knew they were 'stiffs' and was not made muddle-headed by the reference to 'Life as it was always meant to be'. Regardless, Ritter has a worthy opponent in the Court of Boredom. According to Kierkegaard,

> The gods were bored; therefore they created human beings. Adam was bored because he was alone; therefore Eve was created. Since that moment, boredom entered the world and grew in quantity in exact proportion to the growth of population. Adam was bored alone; then Adam and Eve were bored together; then Adam and Eve and Cain and Abel were bored *en famille*. After that, the population of the world increased and the nations were bored *en masse*. To amuse themselves, they hit upon the notion of building a tower so high that it would reach the sky. This notion is just as boring as the tower was high and is a terrible demonstration of how boredom had gained the upper hand. Then they were dispersed abroad, just as people now travel abroad, but they continued to be boring.[7]

So, it's boring up and boring down. Boring ether and boring matter. Boring straight and boring around. And, more than one god. (You would think that this would have made it less boring for them but of course if Kierkegaard's argument is properly followed it immediately becomes apparent that it isn't the more the merrier but the busier the boreder.) But what does any of this mean for justice? There is a maxim, *fiat justitia, ruat caelum* – 'Let justice be done though the heavens fall' – well known as early as 1600 (though God and gods would not, of course, think 1600 to be the slightest bit early). This may be rationalized as the right to judicial handwashing a la Pontius Pilate: 'the judge must do justice according to law, whatever may be the consequences of doing so',[8] 'whatever he or she may think of it'.[9] What if the decision causes the sky to fall? (Not to be confused with a woman falling from the sky which can not, in any event at a certain point in history, occur in Florida on the day of rest for there a chauvinist Chicken Little legislated a special law prohibiting unmarried women from parachuting on Sunday or she shall risk arrest, fine, and/or jailing.[10]) Ah, Chicken Little! Is the sky really falling? If a god is the ultimate judge who decides according to a divine law, we might conclude with Kierkegaard had Kierkegaard been whimsical and wicked that she or he might still be bored enough to cause the sky to fall on all this boringness. When it comes to law, it seems, Chicken Little is not crying wolf (or fire)! Chicken Little is telling it not like it is but how it has to be. And Chicken Little is, in effect, pointing out the possibility of something that may prove to be interesting: the destruction of *all* that is boring. Or might this be just as boring as all that has gone before? And what about justice? I think I'll plump for a woman in a parachute showing us her wrinkled bloomers on the Lord's day. And as he looks up Sergeant Friday might say on a Sunday 'Just the facts, ma'am.' And we all know what he means, don't we, as she comes down screaming on his head and missing the cross completely:

> These hysterical women, privileging the expression of emotion over the recitation of relevant detail, are not being good witnesses. They confuse what an event feels like with what it is; they wander off the point into a tangle of irrelevancies. They do not crisply present the sort of evidence that would allow a conscientious detective like Sergeant Friday to catch the criminal. In short, these women are not helpful to the law.[11]

(And all this despite the fact that her panties were starched and a darn sight more fascinating than... Well, they were just a darn sight! and if anything were capable of making the gods laugh it would be they. Is it possible to be bored while laughing? 'Gods are fond of mockery'.[12])

squeezing desire through a sieve

Justice is ambiguous in a way that injustice never can be. (Serving ice cream on cherry pie was once illegal in Kansas.) Or is such a statement simply the measure of how much difficulty we are in? (You are not allowed to walk across a street on your hands in Connecticut.) Should it be the reverse? Injustice is ambiguous in a way that justice never can be. (In Florida, men may not be seen publicly in any kind of strapless gown.) Are we but the sum total of our desires? (In Texas it is illegal to take more than three sips of beer at a time while standing.) Do our desires enslave us and does their satisfaction set us free? (Making the punishment fit the crime: a man is convicted of growing marijuana plants and the judge makes him put a dope plant in a wheelbarrow and push it round and round the courthouse for a whole day.) Or are we only free when we are without desire? (The tomato was once banned after being described as the love-apple.) What do poetry and law have to do with desire? (Biting someone with your natural teeth is 'simple assault', while biting someone with your false teeth is 'aggravated assault': Louisiana.) Does law involve desire in the process of justice? What's hard to press through a sieve? Flesh? (India has a Bill of Rights for cows.) Does poetry involve desire in the process of justice? (There is a mischief rule that prevents people having birthday cakes made into things that other people would not believe.) What goes through a sieve and comes out the other side the same? Water? (In Alabama, community leaders passed an ordinance that makes it illegal for anyone to try and stop a child from playfully jumping over puddles of water.) What we want can be as hard to believe as what we don't. (Those who have taken charge have banned cinema and music and women on the street; words describing laughter and ball games and evening.) Sometimes what we want and what we don't are two different things. (As Nelson Mandela said in his speech from the dock: 'It is an ideal which I hope to live for and to achieve. But if needs be, it is an ideal for which I am prepared to die.') Sometimes they coincide. ('[A]n injustice is tolerable only when it is necessary to avoid an even greater injustice': John Rawls.) So much for getting anywhere, viz, our desire to understand our desires and to do justice to them without recourse to temptation, satisfaction or abandonment. (In Greece there is a law against afternoon naps…) If the price of justice is eternal vigilance, there is no question that the poem tires as easily as the law.

ENDNOTES

1. *Deatons Proprietary Limited v Flew* [1949] CLR (High Court of Australia, On appeal from the Supreme Court of New South Wales) pp370-388.

2. *Petterson v Royal Oak Hotel Ltd* (1947) 48 NZLR 136.

3. Lorraine Code, *Rhetorical Spaces: Essays on Gendered Locations, op cit.*

4. Fernando Pessoa, *op cit*, p267.

5. Friedrich Nietzsche, *Beyond Good and Evil, Prelude to a Philosophy of the Future* (translated and with an Introduction and Commentary by R.J. Hollingdale), Penguin Books, Harmondsworth, Middlesex, England, 1973, p196.

6. Mark Ritter, 'Heaven Will be Boring! *and Other Common Myths, Misconceptions, & Misunderstandings Concerning the Christian Faith*', http://www.geocities.com/darrickdean/miscon.html.

7. Soren Kierkegaard, 'Rotation of Crops' in *Either/Or: A Fragment of Life,* (edited by Victor Eremita and translated by Alastair Hannay), Penguin, 1992, p286.

8. J. Hayne, 'Letting Justice Be Done Without the Heavens Falling', The Fourth Fiat Justitia Lecture, Monash University, 21 March 2001, p1.

9. *Ibid*, p4.

10. 'Laws of America: Strange but True...', *Poetic Justice*, Faculty of Law, UNSW, sometime in the late 80's.

11. Kim Lane Scheppele, 'Just the Facts, Ma'am: Sexualized Violence, Evidentiary Habits, and the Revision of Truth', Vol.37 *New York Law School Law Review,* 1992, pp123-172, p123. Tense in quote changed from past to present.

12. Friedrich Nietzsche, *op cit*, p199.

iv

blindness & appearance,
identity & disguise…

acquitted of being *ivan the terrible*

Is it possible to be acquitted of *being* someone? 'Ivan started as an angel.'[1]
If your name is Ivan – the Russian form of John, God is giving, God is
gracious – and you are terrible, which incidentally is very notable as well
as, or instead of, being very bad, might you be Ivan the Terrible? It seems
that you don't have to be, even if you were in the right place at the right
time and doing the right things to be him. (Though perhaps from the point
of view of the accused – the 'might be *I the T*' – these are the wrong places
and the wrong times, i.e., when it is a bad time to be yourself.) Is this
because Ivan the Terrible is an idea which must be satisfied? Or more than
one idea? Who is Ivan the Terrible? 'Ivan the Terrible was the fallen angel.'[2]
Is there more than one Ivan the Terrible? I have managed in a very short
space of time to find at least two. 'He started as a very wise Tsar and ended
as a devil.'[3] One who was and one who wasn't convicted of being *I the T*.
But were they themselves? And was *himself* Ivan the Terrible? Is it possible
to be convicted of being *someone*? Three Israeli judges ruled that Ukraine-
born John Demjanjuk, 68, was the guard known as 'Ivan the Terrible' at
the Treblinka death camp in Poland during World War II. ('He could now
be given the death penalty when sentence is passed…') Presiding judge
Dov Levine said: "we have concluded unequivocally, without the slightest
doubt…" But even after the guilty verdict Demjanjuk insisted he was not
Ivan.

> In Context: John Demjanjuk was sentenced to death but appealed.
> His conviction was quashed in 1993 by the Israeli Supreme
> Court, after evidence suggested that another Ukrainian was Ivan
> the Terrible. [A third *I the T*?] John Demjanjuk returned to the
> United States, where, in 1998, his citizenship was restored. In
> 2000 he began a civil action for damages of $5m from the US

government. In February 2002 John Demjanjuk's US citizenship was once again revoked. A judge ruled that even if Demjanjuk were not Ivan the Terrible, there was enough evidence to prove he had been a death camp guard. The 81-year-old is appealing against the decision.[4]

If you are acquitted of being someone are you nobody? Or must you be someone else? The other Ivan was born on August 25, 1530 in Moscow. He suffered from poor health, was ignored and his education was neglected. (Or so they say.) In 1547, Ivan was crowned as Tsar – the first Russian ruler to be crowned Tsar and to hold that official title – and married Anastasia Romanov. [The Romanov dynasty ruled Russia from 1613 to 1917 and traces its claim to the throne from their union, through Anastasia's brother Nikitu.]

He was noted for his highly progressive administrative policies'[5] and was happy with his wife who may have been poisoned according to recent forensic tests on her hair which revealed massive amounts of mercury. 'He set up a bodyguard that has been described as Russia's first 'secret police' – the Oprichniki – as a religious brotherhood sworn to protecting God's Tsar. In reality, they became marauding thugs, ready to commit any crime in the Tsar's name. Ivan sentenced thousands to internal exile in far flung parts of the empire. Others were condemned to death; their families and servants often killed as well. Ivan would give detailed orders about the executions, using biblically inspired tortures to reconstruct the sufferings of hell. More than 3,000 people lost their lives in Ivan's attack on Novgorod alone.[6]

The filmmaker, Eisenstein, shows Ivan in the Cathedral with the Last Judgement as backdrop (he had, by the way, gouged out the eyes of the architects of Saint Basil's Cathedral so that nothing as beautiful would ever be built again). History can be a backdrop. Once 'In a fit of rage, Ivan struck his son and heir dead with his staff. Mad with sorrow and guilt, he had a dramatic volte face, posthumously forgiving [makes it sound like he's dead and not that they are dead!] all those he'd executed and paying for prayers to be said for their souls. Before his death, Ivan was re-christened as the monk Jonah and buried in his monk's habit – in the hope of finding ultimate forgiveness.'[7] In the film, 'God keeps silence when Ivan asked him "have I right to kill people for the Great Russia?" and because silence is the answer, Ivan is trying to kill the God,' explains film historian Naum Kleinman.[8] Was he successful? Is God dead? The case, as we see at this 11th hour, is not solved...

9th june, 11am:
in god's spotlight of judgment

Justice: lantern of which light may be concealed. Dark lantern of light. 'Could it be that the dark is the inner movement of words? But truth is not verbal. It is the place words come back to at night.'[9] At night we have the habit of switching on the lights. 'The white light is artificial, and hygienic as heaven.'[10] This was said in a hospital. ('The white sheet, / Pure white as Judgment Day.'[11]) We should think about what we say. About the meanings of 'sterile'. After all it is not what you say but what you say *and* your intersection with history, your people, and your enemies. What are those people with placards saying? Those ones gathered outside the abortion clinic? '...various segments of society struggle to speak for the fetus, to assign it rights and interests that coincide with their own, thus projecting their own needs onto the fetus.'[12] Judgement is the last refuge of conscience. The refuge has a small light burning in its window. '[F]or that my house is the subject place for my refuge, my safety and comfort of my family'.[13] That it may also be a place where a husband procures a stranger to rape his wife 'to punish her for past misconduct'[14] using another's body to 'provide the physical means to that end'[15] cannot be represented in this fictive eloquence. So think about the meaning of 'refuge'. What one does there. One is protected but one may also hide. Judgement thinks to bring things into the light of day yet the light is blinding. Justice is blind, they say, but in truth justice is what is seen. It is judgement that wants to look. Its ordeals are for the unfree. Justice goes on in darkness and avoids the spotlight. If ever glimpsed by those whose words make all connections, live all lives, 'The far-off landscape will bloom / Like a destiny in the vivid light'.[16] And we all know the destiny of all destinies... To disappear![17]

men in drums

STORY ONE: THE MILK CAN

"I sat down to write something and I realized that unless you can find something to latch onto, some meaning, you can't write a word. What would I say? When he was a little boy we put him in a milk can and mum had to pour cooking oil in there to get him back out. Does that say something about how big a milk can is, or how small he was, or that mum was cluey, or that if you're slippery enough you can get out of anything? Or does it simply mean that we were naughty, or as naughty as kids are? And he was little, or at least the littlest of us. For a while anyway because he ended up taller than all us girls. Taller and naughtier. Or that's what we thought. Probably only because we were older and we were girls. And mum was always wagging the wooden spoon at him and saying 'Don't tease the girls.' But he did tease us, he kept teasing us, holding things out of reach, stinging our legs with the end of a rolled up teatowel.

Six months ago he said to me 'Gwen, I've been hearing things' and I said 'God you're a tease Fin.' I couldn't hear him. But *he* kept hearing *them*. And he wasn't teasing.

Later we talked and I listened and as I listened I saw him in the milk can, stuck fast, unable to get out. And later still mum was there, and Hilary, but none of us, not mum or Hil or me could get him out of that can where the voices were echoing and loud and persistent. We poured our love over him like it was oil, wet and warm, but he wouldn't come out. When I sat down to write though, I thought maybe there was another way to look at it. Maybe Fin did get out of what he wanted to. He made his own decision. Hil and I put him in that milk can when he was a little boy, but Fin's life was his own can. He always did what he wanted, what he thought was right and he's asked us to live with that. And we can live with that. But with whatever Fin heard, he couldn't."

§

His ears felt tired from listening for authenticity. At first he'd believed all the noises and had gone looking for them. Like you do. Like we all do. But he'd only found some of them. And not enough to stay happy with what his ears were telling him. All his life he'd had those ears and he'd never had reason to think about them. Now he knew they were out there and he didn't trust them. Put his fingers in them. Shook his head. Stopped believing them.

He went into his workroom to get his bag. The camera. The lenses. The film. His eyes were still O.K., except that things didn't look as good as they somehow used to. People didn't look as happy. As relaxed. Or as innocent. He'd been thinking about it a lot and that seemed to be at the centre of it. Innocence. Before they'd looked like other people whose faces he could see and if he talked to them then the conversation and their faces would follow each other. If he said something nasty they would get angry or sad. If he cracked a joke they'd laugh. If he talked about his work they would look interested or bored. If it was possible to happen, it was possible to foresee. And there was a certain innocence about it. He knew that now. He just wasn't sure any more whether it was his or theirs. And now it was missing. Now he couldn't see what it was that he might be imagining. What they might be imagining. And so he had stopped speaking. Not all of the time, but for most of it. And when he wasn't speaking he was wondering. About innocence. About how we protect the innocent, or at least try to, as if they have an intrinsic right to protection, and as if, and this seemed to follow from the first, as if those who are not innocent are less deserving of consideration and protection. He felt this was wrong, but when he looked at the people – other people – he couldn't trust their smiles, or their frowns, or the way their eyes moved this way or that, and he felt afraid. The fear was all mixed up with wondering what it was he, or they, had lost. With his inability to interpret their rapidly moving features – the noses, eyes, mouths, eyebrows and lips that were thrown together in combinations that defied him. He felt they must be doing it on purpose, couldn't be innocent, because before he had understood their faces. Before he had found in those faces all that a lifetime had taught him to look for there. Now, none of them were telling him what he could see. And though he could see them – through the lens of his camera, or across the table, or out on the street in broad daylight – they were lit by suspicion and shadowed by fear and he made his own picture of them, unrecognizable even to himself.

The phone rang. But he didn't answer it. Might ask himself – some other time – if he even heard it. Or heard not it, but simply the sound. It rang while he went into the yard and came back inside with the hose. It rang while he opened the drawer and took out the stanley knife. It rang while he cut the hose. It rang while he took several screwdrivers from the box under the sink. While he held them in his hands, felt completely and in some complete way the smooth plastic of their handles. Saw yellow and green. Bright tools that are easy to find. It rang – even more loudly – while he ripped several pages from the pad near the phone and while he took a pen from a jar and lay it next to the screwdrivers on the kitchen bench. Red next to yellow and green. It rang while he took his keys from where he'd left them the night before. While he picked up the bag with his gear, grabbed two plums from the bowl shaped like an open book. Small black words of some ceramicist's language painted over its surface. Then glazed. It rang while he put on his jacket then stopped ringing briefly while he looked at the clock. Rang again a split second later while he noticed the time, thought whatever he thought, wished he wasn't doing what he was doing. It rang against the walls, down the hall, at the opening of the front door. And it rang all the way out of the house.

§

His mum's house had a garage. After pushing down the locks, he unscrewed all the handles and window-winders from the inside of the car doors. Then he panicked. Then he heard the phone. Still ringing.

§

The woman stood on the rostrum, her two daughters supporting her. One on either side. Like bookends. Profiles of her own face at twenty-nine and thirty-five. Between her fingers she held something she still did not believe, but was going to read. A note. Did he leave a note? Not a photograph. Or a painting. Or some graffiti. But a note. Left on the windscreen of the car like a parking ticket. "The one thing I think of is the surf. And Gwen's and Hil's four feet sticking up out of a wave. I knew they were in the wave. But I couldn't see them. I can't see anyone anymore. Everyone's in the wave. No-one else can see the feet. How do you explain feet to people who can't see them?"

DECISION:
When a man is in a drum, you cannot see the man.
Suicide (felon of itself), fantastic and imprecise.

STORY TWO: 3 CLEARED IN DRUM DEATH

> A white farmer and his two sons have been acquitted on charges of murdering a black farm labourer who died after they sealed him in a steel drum for a day.
> The labourer, Steven Phuti, suffocated after being put in a 4,000-litre steel drum, whose ends were then sealed with

concrete with steel pipes welded over them, a court in Rustenburg, 150 km northwest of Johannesburg, was told yesterday.

The 60-year-old farmer, Christian Pretorius, and his two sons, aged 22 and 15 pleaded not guilty.

Their defence counsel said Phuti had been held because they suspected him of stealing cattle.

Mr Justice D.J. Le Roux ruled that the death was not due to the actions or negligence of the accused.[18]

DECISION:

When men put another man in a drum you cannot see them do it.
Murder is so fantastic that it is hardly ever seen and so precise that its terms are hardly ever met.

caught on film:
the utter seriousness of seeing the soul

You know, the courts might not work anymore, but as long as
everyone is videoing everybody else, justice will be done.[19]

A flash of light imprints a lingering image in your eye. Without a boundary,
it's hard to distinguish different shades of grey. Everyone is you and me. I
am a camera. *Recorda sunt vestigia vetustatis et veritatis*. Records are vestiges
of antiquity and truth. *Veritas nihil veretur nisi abscondi*. Truth fears nothing
but concealment. Invisible eyes. A hidden camera photographs a woman in
a supermarket stealing a furry object from a toy display. A private detective
is hired to spy on a man's wife whom the man suspects of adultery. With
a surveillance camera hidden in a teddy bear (also available in wall clocks,
light bulbs, smoke detectors, peep holes and exit signs) the detective
obtains film of the woman sleeping with the bear (she probably would not
have slept with a wall clock, light bulb, smoke detector, peep hole or exit
sign). He did not, however, manage to photograph her dream:

> I was astounded to see the bear standing upright on his hind legs,
> his back against the post to which he was chained, his right paw
> raised ready for battle. He looked me straight in the eye. This
> was his fighting posture. I wasn't sure if I was dreaming, seeing
> such an opponent. They urged me to attack. "See if you can hit
> him!" they shouted. As I had now recovered somewhat from my
> astonishment I fell on him with my rapier. The bear made a slight
> movement with his paw and parried my thrust. I feinted, to
> deceive him. The bear did not move. I attacked again, this time
> with all the skill I could muster. I know I would certainly have
> thrust my way through to a human breast, but the bear made
> a slight movement with his paw and parried the thrust. ...the

bear's utter seriousness robbed me of my composure. Thrusts and feints followed thick and fast, the sweat poured off me, but in vain. It wasn't merely that he parried my thrusts like the finest fencer in the world; when I feinted to deceive him he made no move at all. No human fencer could equal his perception in this respect. He stood upright, his paw raised ready for battle, his eye fixed on mine as if he could read my soul there, and when my thrusts were not meant seriously he did not move.[20]

The wife was tired and in need of sleep and by morning there were ten and a half hours – six hundred and thirty minutes; 37 800 seconds – of film to look through. Despite the fact that she slept naked and had spent a good part of her night parrying thrusts, the private dick himself fell asleep while trawling the tape. (Government experts on security technology have noted that 'monitoring video screens is both boring and mesmerizing' and they have found in experiments that 'after only 20 minutes of watching and evaluating monitor screens, the attention of most individuals has degenerated to well below acceptable levels.'[21]) This left 36 600 seconds for the dick to dream. But what?[22] He wetly dreamed (Extreme CCTV manufactures video surveillance cameras for explosive, wet, and corrosive environments as well as infrared cameras and illuminators for total darkness performance) that he was one of three finalists vying to become chief of the city's police department when a lawsuit came to light just days after reports became public claiming that he was the subject of sexual harassment and abuse allegations from at least five women over a 10 year period. Despite the fact that a district court judge dismissed all 13 lawsuits for lack of merit, he had to abandon his ambitions and get a job as the head warden in a private prison for women offenders. There he rescinded a policy of issuing female prisoners with panties and bras. Instead, they were given one-piece jumpsuits and were forced to expose themselves to video surveillance cameras when using the bathroom.[23] Which was what woke him. He needed to go. Now, he'd fallen asleep at work and his office was in a highrise that employed for its own protection all the latest security on offer. Whilst peeing he glances up and notices a small hole in the centre of the smoke detector that's stuck to the ceiling of the commode.[24] He urinates on his foot. He zips his trousers and climbs up and removes it. Inside he finds a video camera with a transmittal device. Overwhelmed, shocked and mortified he loses his balance due to his sloshy peed on boot and falls on his arse.

So what is the moral of this story? 'God's eyes here on earth'[25] are on everyone? Look before you leak? The bored don't necessarily make the better voyeurs? (Though they may at first be opportunistic lookers.) How about, on film the soul suffers the same fate as its owner — packs on ten pounds and doesn't come off well unless it's fucking the director. We all need the right lighting and a sympathetic audience. We all know that teddy bears are warmer and fuzzier than smoke detectors, so if you have to sleep with an enemy… Meanwhile, always remain suspicious and remember, seeing might be believing but error, artfully coloured, is in many things more probable than naked truth.[26] (Further, we are born into a film already running,[27] and no amount of study or concentration will really help you work out what's going on.)

ENDNOTES

1. Film historian Naum Kleinman, © 1998 WETA, http://www.pbs.org/weta/faceofrussia/timeline/1500/1533-84.html.

2. *Ibid.*

3. *Ibid.*

4. http://news.bbc.co.uk/onthisday/hi/dates/stories/april/18/newsid_2525000/2525057.stm.

5. *Ibid.*

6. *Ibid.*

7. *Ibid.*

8. Film historian Naum Kleinman, *op cit.*

9. Edmond Jabès, 'Journal III', *The Book of Questions,Volume II,* (translated by Rosmarie Waldrop), Wesleyan University Press, University Press of New England, Hanover, 1983, 1984, 1991, p103.

10. Sylvia Plath, 'The Surgeon at 2 a.m.', *Collected Poems,* Faber and Faber, London, 1981, p170.

11. Yehuda Amichai, 'Elegy on the Lost Child', *Yehuda Amichai: A Life of Poetry 1948-1994,* (translated by Benjamin and Barbara Harshav), HarperCollins, 1994, p75.

12. Valerie Mark, 'The Flip Side of Fetal Protection Policies: Compensating Children Injured Through Parental Exposure to Reproductive Hazards in the Workplace', *Golden Gate Law Review*, Vol. 22, 1992, p673.

13. *The Case of the Prerogative of the King in Saltpetre*, Cokes Report, Vol. 12:13.

14. *R v Cogan and Leak,* 1976: 221.

15. *Ibid.*

16. Yves Bonnefoy, from 'The Orangery' ('L'orangerie'), *Early Poems 1947-1959,* (translated by Galway Kinnell and Richard Pevear), Ohio University Press, Athens, 1991, 1992, p125.

17. Eugenio Montale, from 'Cuttlefish Bones', *Collected Poems 1920-1954,* (translated by Jonathan Galassi), Farrar Straus and Giroux, New York, 1998, 2000, p47. ('So disappearing is the destiny of destinies.')

18. AAP, Johannesburg, *Sydney Morning Herald.*

19. Marge Simpson, *The Simpsons,* Television cartoon.

20. Heinrich Von Kleist, 'On the Marionette Theatre' from Heinrich Von Kleist, Charles Baudelaire, Rainer Maria Rilke, *Essays on Dolls,* (translated by Idris Parry and Paul Keegan), Syrens, Penguin Books, London, 1994, pp10-11.

21. American Civil Liberties Union Freedom Network, http://www.aclu.org.

22. The following section paraphrases and merges together some cases found on http://www.notbored.org/camera-abuses.html, the website of New York Surveillance Camera Players; notbored@optonline.net; snail mail: SCP c/o NOT BORED! POB

1115, Stuyvesant Station, New York City 10009-9998.

23. 5 February 2004, Texas City, Texas: 'Scandal erupted in finalist's former dept.' by Alicia Gooden, 2004, *Galveston County Daily News*. Based on the 'real-life' case of Billy Hammitt and merged here with the case of Anthony Morgan.

24. 11 July 2003, Atlanta, Georgia: 'Woman claims she was videotaped in Toys R Us restroom' by the Associated Press.

25. New York Surveillance Camera Players; notbored@optonline.net; snail mail: SCP c/o NOT BORED! POB 1115, Stuyvesant Station, New York City 10009-9998.

26. *Bouvier's 1856 Law Dictionary.* 2 Co. 73.

27. Said by a woman, must hire a private dick to find her!

V

interpretation & certainty,
animality & justification...

the hue & cry

Process of pursuing with horn and with voice... ('capture the sound of speech close up ... and make us hear in their materiality, their sensuality, the breath, the gutturals, the fleshiness of the lips, a whole presence of the human muzzle'[1]) ...all felons and such as have dangerously wounded another... ('that the voice ... be as fresh, supple, lubricated, delicately granular and vibrant as an animal's muzzle ... it caresses, it grates, it cuts, it comes'[2]) ...all those who join in a hue and cry are justified in apprehending the person pursued... ('unleashed attack-phrases'[3] as the violence of the courts is justified by reasons and by collective process) ...even though it should turn out that he is innocent (like the innocence of the raped? the animal? the child?; the innocence of us all?) ...maliciously or wantonly to raise a hue and cry is a misdemeanour and ground for a civil action (as the action of pursuing was itself not an action that was civil, sadly resulting in the wretched but excited pulling of arms and legs until they came off and were stomped on by a crowd, itself an innocent overexcited animal taking part in a larger 'of-which-it-was-not-in-control' process...) ...old common law process ('the commonsense of the community, crystallized and formulated by our forefathers'[4]) ...'from the very beginning of the game, world, public space, body, being-in-common, extension of the soul–'[5] ('from one lip to the other, from you to me'[6]) ...an outcry calling upon all to pursue one who is to be made prisoner (as 'a community can last only at the level of the intensity of death; it falls apart as soon as it fails the particular greatness of danger'[7]) and pain.

"do not open oven door for at least ten minutes" a recipe concerning the poison formerly used for the judicial ordeal

A wife disapproved of her husband's actions. Being of a fair disposition she selected a jury of her peers. To them she put, without bias and in a spirit of mimicry, pivotal examples of his behaviour. 'On Monday he told me that I do not act as he expects a woman to act.' On hearing this her equals replied: '...we are told not that Femininity is a false entity, but that the women concerned are not feminine'.[8] 'On Tuesday he flung his dinner at my head.' On hearing this there was a collective gasp: 'Isn't Tuesday your hair salon day?' 'On Wednesday he smashed my sphere – the most perfect sphere ever made by humans.' Her peers responded: 'We have, most of us, lost a child and empathize completely and perfectly.' 'On Thursday he insisted I belonged to him and made me his. This was not entirely unpleasant yet still I resent it.' This tidbit was given great consideration before being answered: 'Passion is the declared basis of madness and there is a recognized linkage between madness and animality.' 'On Friday he reached out and snapped the little finger on my hand saying he mistook it for a chicken bone.' The women of the jury all clucked. 'On Saturday he owned me again, many times.' As a single voice there came the reply: '... we cannot enter the struggle as objects in order to later become subjects'.[9] 'On Sunday he rested and during this virtual equilibrium it dawned on me that with him I am always alone and that even with him I am always alone.' With this the jury unanimously concurred and stood vowing to reach a decision in order '...that the souls of women may no longer be the only unadorned and neglected things.'[10]

After a short time well utilized the jury returned to the woman's kitchen (where the evidence was heard) and stated that they did not feel it was necessary to hear the husband justify his actions and that they would not call him as a witness when all he was likely to do was defend himself. Their leader handed the wife a piece of paper with their verdict recorded upon it:

RECIPE FOR CREAM OR CUSTARD PUFFS

(EXTRACTED FROM *THE COMMONSENSE COOKERY BOOK, BOOK 1*, METRIC EDITION[11])

INGREDIENTS

1 quantity choux pastry

Cream or custard

(having all taken afternoon tea with you we are aware that you know the recipes for these by heart)

Icing sugar

Poison formerly used for the judicial ordeal (powdered)

METHOD

1. Grease scone tray.
2. Place small spoonfuls of pastry onto pan, allowing room to spread.
3. Bake in a hot oven, 220-250 degrees C, for 1/2 hour or longer, gradually reducing heat. Do not open oven door for at least 10 minutes.
4. When cooked, cool on a cooler.
5. When cool, open near the top.
6. Fill with whipped cream or custard.
7. Sprinkle with icing sugar mixed with poison powder.

The wife chose the cream over the custard. And she mused while mixing the final ingredients in her bowl that there are those (like her husband, for example) who might think the sugar is the icing on the cake.

POSTSCRIPT: As the years passed she enjoyed a relaxing and solitary life, a life filled with cooking and delightful afternoon teas. And as the instrument eventually overtakes the person, she, herself, came to resemble a cream puff, though certainly not one dusted with poison.

revealing certainty for something it wasn't
(or 'a species of prison')

> I read all the time and I often believe what I read while I'm
> reading it ... [though] ... I've been trying to train myself for
> thirty or forty years not to believe anything anyone tells me. [12]

Those I most like to disbelieve and disobey are the certain: 'To quote
from memory the man himself, he said something along the lines of "the
difference between *Woman* and *I*, is that *I* know what I am saying" – language
is man's, full stop.' [13] Certainty is a kind of injury; a species of prison.
Certainty wounds possibility and imprisons the imagination. *Ought. Shall
be. Therefore. Ought. Shall be.* Certainty is a halt, an end. Certainty is finality.
A dead body. Corpus. A body of literature or law. Not to be doubted.
Resolved. Fixed. Inevitable. As in, there is a certain *kind* of reading: 'the
question of belief or disbelief, in the intellectual sense [as opposed to the
emotional sense] never arises when we are *reading well*'. [14] What might
I think is meant when reading about 'a certain person' (implying some
degree of contempt?), 'a lady of a certain age' (one no longer young?),
or someone 'in a certain condition' (euphemism for pregnant?). Is my
reading of a sufficient quality if I interpret this to mean that certain groups
of people approve of certain groups of people and not of others? And
further, that certain people's perception of reality influences what they
perceive? Let us see:

BY THE CURRENT ELSEWHERE
(for Virginia Woolf who valued reading)

A phrase blew through the room where I sat on my own. I saw blowing with it, voices from another room. And from the garden where she stood, still as a clothesline after rain, a question "Why were you getting your picture taken?"

"Because I had my hat on."

And a child's voice – it was Daniel – "Sometimes we change our hose and plug it somewhere else."

"Where?" asked the question.

"Some special place" said the child. "They scare you because you didn't see them. And they tickle me. I saw one go for a swim."

Without going to the window I saw bits of the child, through the lattice fence, like a jigsaw, a blue eye, an ear-lobe. He took one of the others by the hand and was pointing as they both bent over. "Some spiders grow plants for you" he said in a windy little voice, full of teaching, "and they spit out water."

There was a spider under the corner of the desk where I sat. It was in a small puddle of sun – basking. It really could have been blowing bubbles if I looked closer. But I didn't.

Instructions were still coming from the garden. "I kill them with my legs. I step on them. And they don't bite me because I've got my shoes on. And then I drop a lump of wood on them."

Stay where you are spider, I warned, there's asylum in my desk. Looking down at the book I read, " *'OTHER THEFTS – REMINISCENCES OF A CITY CHILDHOOD', One day, I was sitting in front of my house, reading and ruffling the back of the cat, when a dog ripped my foot off. I imagined at first it would be like tiredness, like lies, like other thefts... but it gave me nightmares that were already true.*" I turned to the very front of the book. I wondered if it was a true story. Finding nothing, I turned to the back. Not meaning to, I saw the last line.

The child had found an old pen in the garden. "It doesn't work" said the adult, in the way that someone grown up says that kind of thing, and then

78

again "It doesn't work."

The smaller voice conspired "Once all the ink runs out on to the paper in writing then the pen's finished."

So's the story, I said. I couldn't read it now that I had seen the last line. What did it mean anyway? I'd have it in mind all the way through every page, every chapter. There was no point now for me to follow the careful building, the gathering of stones, the stacking, the expected becoming the unexpected – I knew what the house looked like finished, and in fact had seen it demolished. And there was no way it was a true story – not with a last line like that. Closing the book I looked at the cover and the sub-title *'reminiscences of a city childhood'*. That was there certainly to give it the 'feeling' of being a true story, and there was a photograph of a city – and yes it was a real city, a very particular and existing city for sure – on the cover.

The author was claiming to live, or to have lived, in that city – by putting that picture – no 'photo' – on the cover of the book. If you looked closely you could no doubt see the author, when the author was a child of course, sitting there in that city, on a footpath, being passed and brutalized by a savage dog. But, just like spiders spitting water, you would only see it if you looked close enough. I didn't. You could only look close enough in this situation by reading the book and because when reading a book I *never* read the last line first, then here, where I had read the last line before really even being in the act of reading the book, I felt a loyalty in the converse and could not therefore read the book.

Which all meant that I now had to find something else to do. My intention, and desire, had been to spend the morning reading, and yes reading that particular book. It was new (something which unaccountably and probably unjustifiably had also made me think it could have been a true story, as if being modern, current, made it somehow more 'true', like 'news' or a 'recount') and a gift. Yesterday it was my birthday and someone had given me the book and had written in the front 'for all your future not yet used', as if it would take me the rest of my life to read it. Well, it hadn't. It had taken me two seconds – I had finished it – and it was finished for me in a way that was beyond all contention, the last line rule being a singular kind of rule was a rule without exceptions – before I had barely begun.

The voices outside were getting further and further away "…a cat had that many claws" said the child.

Do all cats I wondered, have that many claws? And how many was that many? How many claws do cats have? Some have none. On a program on television the other night were cats who lived in high-rise buildings in cities, who had been de-clawed so that they couldn't scratch, among other things, their owners or their owners' furniture.

Barely heard said the child "Sometimes I sleep on the furniture, when it's dark."

There was a certain amount of synchronicity around today, I thought. That would please one of the professors I had had at the university. I hadn't thought of him in years. Maybe, he too was thinking of me at this very moment. I decided it was perfectly possible. He lived in the city where the university still was.

The author's city was still spread out on the desk before me. Was it full of de-clawed cats in highrises? They would not stand much chance 'clawless' against foot-eating dogs. But perhaps they were never allowed outside their highrise apartments, and certainly their owners – after having gone to the trouble and expense, I imagined it would be expensive, of de-clawing them – would not let foot-eating dogs in. But what if one of the clawless cat-owners had a foot-eating dog-owner for a friend. But, no, in such cities they would choose their friends carefully. People with de-clawed cats would not be friends with people with foot-eating dogs, whom in turn I imagined would not be friends with people with feet.

Then I remembered – the author, or the narrator, who lost the foot on the footpath, had been sitting with a cat. Maybe the dog mistook the foot for the cat, had in fact been after the cat all the time and so wasn't really describable, definable even, as a foot-eating dog, but was in fact a cat-eating dog who simply ate a foot by accident. Regardless, that cat on the path getting its back ruffled would not have been de-clawed because it was not in a highrise but on a footpath. And perhaps that is precisely the explanation for why the dog ate the foot and not the cat. Because the cat had claws and thus stood a chance against the dog and its savagery. But did the dog go for the cat and lose and take the foot as a second choice, to save face perhaps, or did the dog immediately size up that this cat was indeed not one of those defenceless de-clawed cats that sit in highrises and was therefore better avoided and so battle was never joined with the cat at all, but was from the very start done with the foot? But then again, was the foot-eating dog in fact exactly, and just, that – a dog that eats feet and not, never, cats. In which case someone with a de-clawed cat or even a cat with all its faculties could be friends with someone who owned a foot-eating dog. Provided of course that the dogs only interest in the cat was of a benevolent type. This is no way helped with a new quandary that had just occurred to me – the owners of foot-eating dogs, did they have any feet themselves? Or did they train the dogs to leave *their* feet alone? That didn't make sense to me because I thought it would not be good public relations to own a dog that ate any feet – one's own or somebody else's, so if you were going to train a dog to leave your your own feet off the menu, wouldn't it make sense to at the same time convince it that all feet tasted indescribably bad and were better left on the ends of people's legs. Maybe these kinds of dogs were just plain untrainable – a natural instinctive wild savagery – and had a hunger for feet, for juicy toes, nibbly narrow ankles, and only left the feet on their owners, so that the owners could continue to take them for walks, where they could exercise of course, but where they could also come by other people's feet to eat. And so their owners could walk to the shops to buy them food (which is very close in spelling to 'foot', coincidentally – not lost on the dogs I'm sure – perhaps they are dogs that were confused from an early age by their owners calling 'food' and they thought it was 'foot') … anyway as I was saying, so their owners could walk to the shops to buy them food when there is a temporary shortage of feet around.

At this point in my reverie, a smell like a bit of fresh air curled around my ear and up over the top of my head. It lightly lifted the hair closest to my scalp and made me take a deep breath in. This breath was like a mouthful of birds, fluttering, fluttering, and contained trees and light and a gemmy sky. I was sure it would have nothing in common with the concrete breezes that would have been felt by the author as a child in the city on my desk. My smell here was keen and sharp and ticklish. The city smell would have been oily and dirty and lubricated. A smell of livelihood under-cover-of business, a smell of machinery and money and time. A vigilant, gut-churning sickly smell of tiredness and new school uniforms.

A smell to strip the skin off your hands.

A smell of headaches, of waiting, and exhaustion. I closed my eyes and imagined the small author on the path in front of the house. Close to the road and to puddles of grease dripping from cars on to the bitumen. And the cat's back that is being ruffled has a dark streak of grease along it, as the backs of city cats often do, from rubbing themselves against the underside of cars as if against the belly of a giant mechanical smelly mother. Here, I thought, maybe claws aren't the only criterion by which cat-eating dogs decide not to eat cats, or in fact to make them choose to change from cat-eating to foot-eating dogs permanently – maybe the cat was as big as a tree-stump. Maybe it stunk. Then again, feet are notorious for stinking! Obviously, individual dogs would decide which stink they liked and which they didn't. Like I hate liver but love licorice and have never minded the smell of the past, but abhor that of inconvenience.

And curiosity? – that has a smell. The kind that makes you certain you are going to sneeze, but only lasts until you do. Suddenly I wanted a name. Just a name of someone in this city on the desk in front of me. This city that was sharing the room where I sat alone. If I could have just one name, then I would no longer be alone and perhaps the problem of what to do with my now unexpectedly vacant morning would be solved. But I would only open the book once. I was not going to read it so there was no excuse for me to go ferreting around inside of it for this and that. One opening, one name was all I was allowed. So I crossed my fingers and there – page 106 – no need to go reading about all over the place, there she was *"lying face-down on the bed, her accent hidden in sleep."* I tried not to make any noise, but the pages rustled and she rolled over and opened her eyes. She had those brilliant golden kind of eyes, that are in the daylight, molten and cooling.

"Gabina?" I said and she shook her black curly hair away from her face.

"I don't know where my name comes from" she said. "But my grandmother was Gabina. And she's dead. So I'm the only Gabina in the world I think."

"It's a beautiful name, *I think*" I said very honestly, "and at least, well I would guess anyway, that you are the only Gabina in this city."

"That's true" she said. "I am. But it is a foreign city for me. The author, the child out there on the path in front of the house, is very much at home here, but I know little of it. People here say my name as if they have wonderment rolling from the ends of their tongues. I get asked a lot of questions and they do not always understand my replies – my accent is very heavy and the author has not let me change it."

"At least, I suppose, when there is 'Gabina', there on the page, you are there with it and they can look from one to the other, from your name to your brilliant golden eyes and do a little equation."

She looked. "Names" she said.

"Names" I said "are the closest we come to understanding a language we do not speak. Many seem to have no meaning and perhaps that is why we unquestioningly allow them to accompany a particular individual, to become that person."

"Ga - bi - na" I read and she did nothing while she waited for me to finish.

"I'm not allowed to do anything" she explained "until you've gone that far along and read what I have done."

"Don't you get impatient?" I asked. And she laughed as if I had opened my hands and a beautiful insect had flown out and startled her.

"Which would you prefer?" she began, "firstly, for there to be the possibility that you could be undone – destroyed even – by a mere chance. So all may be well forever, unless of course the one in a million happens – the chance happening happens. Nothing else can cause you harm – apart from this occurrence you are invincible. So you are in the hands of fate. Very likely to remain unthreatened, but there is always the possibility, the thing over which you have no control."

Watching her I waited. I felt like I was standing on one leg.

"Or" she went on, "on the other hand, you can be undone if a certain act is done. So you are invincible only if you make sure that this single thing never occurs. Here, you are less in the hands of fate, than in your own hands. You must make certain that this thing is never done, but no chance encounter is capable of undoing you."

"Which would I prefer?" I repeated her words.

"Yes" she said. "Take your pick, but remember, in the first scenario the chance incident is something that is quite unlikely, maybe even improbable, but you are in a lottery – if it will happen there is nothing you can do to stop it. But in the second case, the occurrence is perhaps something that could happen quite easily – it is probable, but here, if you act appropriately, and at the right time, you can stop it. Vigilance – eternal vigilance – is required."

"I am not going to feel safe" I said.

"We, none of us, ever feel safe" she agreed.

"Are you trying to let me know where you are?" I asked, realizing that I was nearing the bottom of the page and had promised to read only that one page, not to turn that page, not to read the book since I had read the last line.

"You are the one who knows where I am" she said, "and where I'm going. I knew it as soon as I opened my eyes. You woke me. It is obvious from your refusal to choose between the two situations I offered that you have read the end of this book. And that is why now I do not feel well. In fact I feel ill and must lie back down."

"Please don't" I said but my eyes skimmed to the very bottom of the page where I saw the words, *"…her tiredness was like that of a hibernating animal, buried beneath great boulders on a mountainside. Indeed, it would be dangerous to…"*, and the page finished.

"You were not meant to wake me" I heard her whisper, or at least I think it was her. There was no way for me to find out, unless I read on – and I had promised not to – and I knew anyway that even if I did read on I would find what I didn't want to find. She was right, none of us are safe. For me the story had been undone by a chance encounter with the last line, and I had been the undoing of her through my lack of vigilance – there had been no need to wake her, no need to open the book, just for a name.

Or was it in fact the other way round – could I have avoided reading the last line, and was my encounter with her fated, because if I hadn't read the last line I would have read the book and encountered her anyway?

Regardless, at the point when I opened the book the second time I really should have been quite happy here in the room of my own. There were many things I could have done – I could have tidied up, or had a sleep, chosen another book (and not been so picky) or even, even, I could have written a story of my own. Would it be worth writing though? Especially if there were people around like me, careless – or unlucky? – who read the last line first, even if by accident – and then couldn't read it?

But I had chosen to wake her, I had seen her golden eyes, like idolatrous Gods, I had destroyed her. Destroyed her story, or at least her part of it. I thought of opening the book back up, of blotting from my mind those last lines, of telling her a lie – that I knew nothing...

A voice from the garden was coming back towards the room "I think we should put all the things we found along here" and I heard it lining things up, "a pen, a rock, a jungle, a piece of water..."

"We can make up a story about them" said the adult.

Typical I said aloud, and didn't open the book. There was a breeze blowing again. The things I had wanted to say, indeed my thoughts, had been taken, by the current, elsewhere...

POSTSCRIPT: No certainty here.

> [M]orevoer, in light of the Disobedience text ...[the]... strategy involves the self in a literalization of the gap between saying and doing. ... [equating two worlds] the "ideal crystalline" one and the "supposedly real" one, with saying and doing, respectively -- This oscillation as a line of escape from perpetually false forms and discourses to "fundamental justice" which is at some point embodied in the act of writing itself, which is only a vehicle for self-realization and coming to terms with "death and responsibility", or "not believing and telling the truth as it comes up"...[15]

CERTAINTY: 1. In which there is most opportunity and potential for uncertainty. 2. Should be rarer than it is. 3. Only works if it's your own.
{See UNCERTAINTY}

UNCERTAINTY: Hesitating before doubt.[16]

there is nothing like an unfinished bridge

The loss of a testicle is a misadventure, but there is nothing like an unfinished bridge. It may be that you are required to prove the cause of death of the testicle – the vas like wet spaghetti – but a bridge that goes halfway to somewhere is proof only of psychology. One testicle can still provide scrotal support while the poor almost-bridge is like a train of thought become lost.

Take the testicle's loser. 'The fact that such a situation was generally regarded as unimportant to the world at large whilst he was overwhelmed by its significance in his life caused him to be both deeply distressed and extremely angry.'[16] Set this fellow side by side with all those on one side of the river over which the bridge is unfinished and with all those on the other. What hangs in the balance? In the former case: A trophy? A testicle? An atrophied testicle that demanded amputation. In the latter: connection; joining; linkage. The one-testicled man – unlike the broken bridge – is uncertain. What does this mean? About the testicle's demise he is certain. The vision of it – going pale, soft and floppy. The feel of it, in handling it. Its shrinking. Its uselessness. It shrank until it was tiny and it died. And then the flighty nurses who think it's a joke. Before the testicle's death he was certain he was a man. Now he is uncertain. The broken bridge, however, is very certain. There it is. It stops. It leads nowhere.

What is at stake?

The unknown is at stake.

For the unbroken bridge – the bridge that spans, that joins this and that but is neither this nor that – *is* uncertainty. It facilitates the possible. Mystery. The broken bridge might not know – never knows – but this is not the unknown. What *isn't* is not unknown but unknowable.

And so our man of the gland resembles the bridge rather than that thing we have been erroneously referring to throughout this essay as 'the unfinished bridge'. (Because he is now certain of many things about which he is mistaken, yet unsure of himself. Who and what he is. If only he has the courage to take such changefulness and doubt firmly in two hands he might find that what issues forth is surprise.) But our unfinished bridge is a thing outside its name. You cannot see what this object is connected to. It experiences and induces a loss of positional sense. Evolution that has become lost in time. A thing that cannot be itself. Flaccid in the truest sense though it might remain erect (and we all know that the state of erection is really horizontal as opposed to vertical!). Truly, the unfinished bridge is not worth speaking about and so ends this...

ENDNOTES

1. Roland Barthes, *The Pleasure of the Text,* (translated by Richard Miller), Hill and Wang, New York, 1975, p67.

2. *Ibid.*

3. Bob Perelman, *The Marginalization of Poetry: Language Writing and Literary History,* Princeton University Press, Princeton, New Jersey, 1996, p105.

4. *Osborn's Concise Law Dictionary,* Seventh Edition by Roger Bird, Sweet & Maxwell, London, 1983, p81.

5. Jean-Luc Nancy, *The Sense of the World,* (translated and with a foreword by Jeffrey S Librett), University of Minnesota Press, Minneapolis, London, 1997 (1993), p67.

6. *Ibid.*

7. Maurice Blanchot, *The Unavowable Community,* (translated by Pierre Joris), Station Hill Press, Barrytown, New York, 1988 (1983), p11, quoting Georges Bataille.

8. Simone de Beauvoir, *The Second Sex,* (translated by H.M. Parshley), Penguin Books, Harmondsworth, Middlesex, England, 1972 (1949), p286.

9. Paulo Freire.

10. Peter Goodrich, 'The City of Ladies (Revisited)', I think!? Though in the interests of unfinishedness and uncertainty there is email correspondence from Peter Goodrich to the author along the lines of 'I am sure I have the reference but I am not sure which article you mean. My guess is that you are thinking of 'Amatory Jurisprudence and the querelle des lois', 2001, vol.76 *Chicago Kent Law Review*, p751 but it could also be 'Law in the Courts of Love: Andreas Capellanus and the Judgments of Love', 1996, vol.48 *Stanford Law Review*, p601. If neither of these then ask me again.' A decision has been made to leave all within the realms of possibility.

11. *The Commonsense Cookery Book, Book 1,* Metric Edition, Compiled by the N.S.W. Public School Cookery Teachers' Association, Angus & Robertson Publishers, London, Sydney, Melbourne, 1970, p148.

12. Alice Notley, 'The Poetics of Disobedience', paper given at a British poetry conference, forwarded on email list: poetics@listserv.acsu.buffalo.edu; originally posted by Anselm Berrigan (30-3-98).

13. Email correspondence (1-4-98) by Bernadette Latour on email list: lesac-net@queernet.org; discussing pschoanalysis and gender difference: 'I am frustrated by a psychoanalytic account which, although freeing us from the tyranny of facts = truth (regardless that often the 'facts' themselves go to disprove the theory…) …especially with Lacan, rebuilds for us an even more secure prison from which we can no longer escape. Language = what makes us human = regulated by the phallus as a privileged signifier and the Law of the Father, and at the end of it Woman does not exist.'

14. I A Richards, *Practical Criticism: A Study of Literary Judgment*, Harcourt Brace & Company, San Diego, New York, London, 1929, p260, emphasis added.

15. Email correspondence (31-3-98) by Robert Hale forwarded on email list: poetics@listserv.acsu.buffalo.edu; he quotes from his review (published in 'Sulfur') of Disembodied Poetics: Annals of the Jack Kerouac School, University of New Mexico Press, 1994 in which appeared Alice Notley's paper 'Epic & Women Poets' and then goes on to add this paragraph in light of Notley's 'The Poetics of Disobedience'.
16. MTC Cronin, *The Dictionary of Rescued Ideas.*
17. Name suppressed.

vi

punishment & reward,
balance & beans…

my speciality is myself

You may judge others only according to your knowledge of yourself.
Tell me now, who among us is guilty and who is unguilty?[1]

I was recently chosen to go on a television gameshow. One of those ones where you are asked questions about your chosen area of expertise. My speciality was myself. The two contestants I was up against were more extroverted. The first one's forte was the agricultural revolution that started in western Asia about 6000 years ago, 'linked with a genetic mutation that enabled certain human beings to drink milk in adulthood'.[2] I was fascinated to learn from this fellow that these (ancient?) paleskins spoke "dairy" languages. The other contestant was a woman who knew all there is to know about clearheadedness. (Apparently the first requirement for it is to be 'rid of any vertigo that may be induced by peering into the abyss of time'.[3]) She was extremely mirthful. But to return to myself... Right from the beginning they (whoever devised the questions for the show) were out to trick me. (It is my belief that most things in life are designed with trickery in mind.) Take a look at their opening questions:

'Are you ever evident to yourself?'
'If so, which bits?'
'And how do you account for that in yourself which you cannot have evidence of?'[4]

Undoubtedly they were expecting me to get stuck in Wittgenstein's mire where part of the 'I' always escapes the 'I's' scrutiny. This did not happen and, after answering this and all other questions correctly, I progressed through to the semi-finals and from there to the grand final. For this auspicious occasion had been invited a guest panel of 'experts' – one from each competitor's field – and it did not surprise me when my doppelganger came out with:

'You obviously think you know yourself well?'

We eyed each other for a good 45 seconds in silence – a long time in television! – after which, of course, I was forced to decline to answer. I knew he'd smirk and he smirked. The person who won the final was extremely well-versed in knocking one's head against a brick wall and when asked if she had a sore head, well, she lied! There is a certain measure of shrewdness required to accept reward, it being the same amount that will counteract an equal degree of punishment already suffered. This I know. My speciality is myself.

a cup of justice

Drinking a cup of Justice... And Justice can taste outstanding.

So goes an ad – USA – for fairly-traded gourmet coffee. Fragrance: team spirit. Appearance: *sub colore juris*. Recommendation: Universal Declaration of Human Rights. Verdict? Full of beans! So many good reasons to drink it. For a lift! Regularity? Just don't overdo it! Too much Justice and you'll be up all night. (No doubt thinking about what might not be a good thing.)

balancing butterflies with butcher's meat:
of course it's really a contest!

Two little recounts:

ONE:

A bitter dispute has broken out between Aeschylus and Euripides, for dead poets, it appears, are not immune from those jealousies and rivalries that plague their living counterparts. As Aristophanes recounts this episode in his farcical play *The Frogs*, what occasions the dispute is a certain dining privilege – a chair by Pluto's side – a privilege long enjoyed by Aeschylus, but which Euripides, new arrival in the underworld, now fancies his due. And so the battle lines are drawn and the poets stand before Dionysus, taunting each other and hacking away at each other's poetry, until, after some lapse of time, an enormous pair of scales is brought out to settle the dispute. "Poetry will be measured by the pound, ... weighed in scales like so much butcher's meat," Aristophanes tells us, and the heavier one will be declared the winner. Three times the poets go to the scales, throwing in their respective lines, and each time Aeschylus wins hands down, for, unlike Euripides, who speaks only of "light and feather-brained" things (such as persuasion), Aeschylus has wisely gone in for the heavy topics. In one line, for instance, "Two chariots and two corpses he heaved in. / A hundred gypsies couldn't hoist them." It is not much of a contest, after all."[5]

TWO:

There is another curious scrap of possible evidence concerning the existence of some concept of a *post-mortem* judgement in pre-Hellenic religion. In certain Mycenaeaen tombs miniature scales or balances, with the figure of butterflies, have been found.

> Since the butterfly could symbolize the soul in later Greek thought, and since the balances are too fragile for practical use, it has been thought by some scholars that belief in *psychostasia* or the weighing of the soul is thereby indicated.... Balances could symbolize the apportioning of fates to living men: thus in the *Iliad* Zeus is represented as weighing in the golden balances the fates of Achilles and Hector at their fatal encounter. On the other hand, the fact that the Mycenaean balances have been found in tombs suggest that they had some mortuary significance.... In such speculation we may also wonder whether the Egyptian belief in the weighing of the heart of the deceased had any influence here; for Egyptian influence can be traced in many other aspects of Cretan and Mycenaean culture.[6]

Now, let's conflate them and weigh the poem against the soul.

THREE:

They each have four letters.

They are each a noun.

In the face of death, neither should collapse.

To those unused to truth, they can be mistaken for one another.

They are each often attributed in origin to what does not exist: the poem to inspiration; the soul to God.

One must find one's own way to them.

They cannot be explained.

Both invite scorn.

Both treat scorn with indifferent grace.

In life they are of such dubious necessity that they are largely ignored which is laughable as it is necessity just the same.

One meaning of 'soul' is the lungs of a goose. A poem might be anything harmonious or satisfying, which things, of course, its lungs might be to a goose.

What wins: what's lighter or what's heavier?

What outweighs or what is outweighed?

It is almost certain that neither the poem nor the soul would attempt to outweigh the other.

Such slight movements. What is the scale doing? Can you see?

Such balance. Such beauty.

Both would without doubt poke out the eye of the beholder.

hearts, feathers, & pebbles:
the ubiquitous desire to weigh & measure

More Judgement Scenes! Borges, our guide to the imaginary, tells us of the *Egyptian Book of the Dead* and the Tibetan *Bardot Thödol*. In both texts, before a jury of deities, some with the heads of apes, there is a symbolical weighing of evil and good deeds:

> In the *Book of the Dead,* a heart and a feather are weighed against each other, "the heart representing the conduct or conscience of the deceased and the feather righteousness or truth". In the Bardo Thödol, white pebbles and black pebbles are placed on either side of the balance.
>
> The Tibetans have demons or devils who lead the condemned to the place of purgation in a hell-world; the Egyptians have a grim monster attending their wicked, an Eater of the Dead.
>
> The dead man swears not to have caused hunger or sorrow, not to have killed or to have made others kill for him, not to have stolen the food set aside for the dead, not to have used false weights, not to have taken the milk from a baby's mouth, not to have driven livestock from their pasturage, not to have netted the birds of the gods.
>
> If he lies, the forty-two judges deliver him to the Eater, "who has the head of a crocodile, the trunk of a lion, and the hinder parts of a hippopotamus". The Eater is assisted by another animal Babaí, of whom we know only that he is frightening and that Plutarch identifies him with the Titan who fathered the Chimera.[7]

Hmmm. I think I'd like to take up these 'false weights'. What is a false weight? How might such a thing exist? It strikes me that a weight will weigh what it weighs – even if that weight changes (it appears, for example, that I'm quite a lump on Io, one of the moons of Jupiter, whereas on Mercury and Mars I'm not much more than one-third of my Earth-weight) – and that the lie lies with the weigher. 'Sometimes the scale pans may weigh correctly, but the balancer is off.'[8] What does this tell us? That there are those who would like to take you for a ride. Who would have us believe that our hearts can be equated with pieces of meat of similar size and mass. Would you be fooled? Would you be tempted to go along? Don't be sluggish of mind. 'If you are in a spaceship far between the stars and you put a scale underneath you, the scale would read zero. Your weight is zero. You are weightless.'[9] Tell this to the falsifiers the next time they come at you with their weights and balances:

> I, who was King of Salt at the seashore,
> Who stood without a decision at my window,
> Who counted the steps of angels,
> Whose heart lifted weights of anguish
> In the horrible contests'[10],
> I weigh the nothing that you weigh, that we all weigh when gravity
> turns its back on us. Even that someone who put a pineapple together,
> viz:
> 'He sees it in this tangent of himself.
> And in this tangent it becomes a thing
> Of weight, on which the weightless rests: from which
>
> The ephemeras of the tangent swarm, the chance
> Concourse of planetary originals,
> Yet, as it seems, of human residence.
>   . . .
> He must say nothing of the fruit that is
> Not true, not think it, less. . . .[11]

102

There are worse fates than being eaten by the mongrels of the gods. Your tricks are all symptoms of your discomfort with *nought*. Work backwards from the denial of denial of justice. Get out your cheeky pans but know, on each side of conscience is a practice.

ENDNOTES

1. Kahlil Gibran, *Sand & Foam*, Brolga Publishing Pty Ltd, 2004 (1927), p42.

2. Nigel Calder, *Timescale ~ An Atlas of the Fourth Dimension*, Chatto & Windus, The Hogarth Press, London, 1984, p90.

3. *Ibid*, p71.

4. A slight rewording of 'Am I ever evident to myself? If so, which bits? And how do I account for that in myself which I cannot have evidence of?' from Margaret Davies, *Asking the Law Question*, The Law Book Company Limited, Sydney, 1994, p70.

5. Wai Chee Dimock, *Residues of Justice: Literature, Law and Philosophy*, University of California Press, Berkeley and Los Angeles, 1997, p1.

6. S.G.F. Brandon, *The Judgement of the Dead: The Idea of Life after Death in the Major Religions*, Charles Scribner's Sons, New York, 1967 (quoted in David Meltzer, *Death: An Anthology of Ancient Texts, Songs, Prayers, and Stories*, North Point Press, San Francisco, 1984, p213).

7. Jorge Luis Borges, *The Book of Imaginary Beings*, (trans. Norman Thomas di Giovanni in collaboration with the author), Penguin Books, (1967, 1969) 1974, pp54-55.

8. Jalal al-Din Rumi, Maulana, 'If You Want to Live Your Soul', *The Soul of Rumi: A New Collection of Ecstatic Poems*, (Translations, Introductions and Notes by Coleman Barks), HarperCollins, San Francisco, 2001, p236.

9. 'Your Weight on Other Worlds', http://www.exploratorium.edu/ronh/weight.

10. Yehuda Amichai, 'God Full of Mercy', *Yehuda Amichai: A Life of Poetry 1948-1994*, (translated by Benjamin and Barbara Harshav), HarperCollins, 1994, p31.

11. Wallace Stevens, 'Someone Puts a Pineapple Together', from 'Three Academic Pieces', *The Necessary Angel: Essays on Reality and the Imagination*, Vintage Books, Alfred A Knopf and Random House, New York, 1942, pp83-84.

vii

irresponsibility & purpose,
drifting & death...

her refusal to hand over the foetus…[1]
to those quoting from a *malignant letter to the unborn*[2]

Dear Foetus,

As T. S. Eliot describes your laugh,[3] I guess you are in a relatively good position despite those judges who would classify you as an 'alien' to the womb.[4] They do this to deny immigrants entry to this, the mother country.

We, who believe in asylum *and* in the right to abortion ('foetus' and 'products of procreation'), are getting in touch to offer any legal assistance that may be necessary to counter their ('child' and 'little baby')[5] malignancy. The message they have sent to you should serve as a warning about the world you will try to enter.

And you, 'You must be the change you wish to see in the world.'[6] Although you have been genetically engineered 'The person who discovered the law of love was a far greater scientist than any of our modern scientists. Only our explorations have not gone far enough and so it is not possible for everyone to see all its workings.'[7]

We look forward to your arrival: 'the life that is born every day the death that is born every life',[8] knowing in the meantime that 'The foetus is uniquely situated to perform this role as a symbol of social fears and conflicting mores in a rapidly changing society.'[9] (Especially when the direct and uncomfortable result of irresponsibility on someone's part.)

With all best wishes and in anticipation

Those born

P.S. Just to let you know, we have recently heard about the 'supposed opacity of the womb'. Be careful while adrift. Keep an eye out.

death doesn't help

Desperate to enforce death? It seems that one ought to be sane in order to be put to death. But there is a new law in Arkansas where a prisoner on death row went mad and therefore could no longer be legally popped off. Legislation was promptly passed to enable this fellow to be medicated to the point of sanity whereupon, sedated, he could be (sanely?) executed.[10]

This essay is a little admonition to those who think death – for the dead – is a solvent to clean away legal blemishes. Sort of like maxing your credit card and then topping yourself. Unfortunately, law's dirt is a kind that sticks. (After all, we all know there's more to 'death and taxes' than we've been told.) I will quote from two poems of mine where I relay information found in 'real-life' court cases:

FROM: IN THE STYLE OF A GREAT POET,
RATHER THAN AN EPILOGUE

I read about a court case
where tendered in evidence
were words spelled out by a ouija board
– 'stephen young done it' –

and even better
the judge described this
as an unsworn statement from the deceased

FROM: SURVIVAL

"The defendant, by answering, proves he is
alive; and when he avers in his answer
that he is dead, he is not to be
believed."[11]

Now, before we discuss law's relationship to death and the dead, it's necessary to define terms.

The distance between *death* and *dead* is not only much greater than several consonants, but enormously greater than that which lies between *life* and *death*. Life and death go together: while doing the first we invent, as an idea, as a concept, the second. Dead, on the other hand, is not 'on the other hand'. (What is it they say? There is only an alternative to death?) It is quite undoable and further, quite untheoretical. Try 'being dead'. No wonder the defendant, even the dead defendant, cannot be believed. The law will take him to task regardless. Surprising, then, that the ouija board evidence wasn't found to be hearsay? But no, you would be misled if you tried to argue that this is an example of *dead* moving closer to *life* – the voice of the dead being *heard* by the living. It is, in fact, a complete inability to recognize and acknowledge deadness by the interpolation of an object, here the speaking board, between the living and the dead. More, the object is imbued with life, just proving how impossible it is for us to really understand what dead means or is.

What evidence exists for this? Death has aesthetics. Death might be attributed a persona. One might seek it (or at least roads that lead to it[12]). Death scares us. Dead, though, is just dead. No amount of teasing and prodding comes up with anything. Law, therefore, must knock it on the head quick smart. The law doesn't like things around which it cannot explain and which it cannot subsume. Remember our beautiful Agamben quote:

> Law is made of nothing but what it manages to capture inside itself through the inclusive exclusion of the *exceptio*: it nourishes itself on this exception and is a dead letter without it. In this sense, the law truly 'has no existence in itself, but rather has its being in the very life of men.[13]

Ah, the *dead letter*. Despite such threats, Law is, perhaps, the only system

110

that attempts to make dead rub shoulders with life. Religion, contrary to expectations, doesn't do this. It has its back to dead as it both threatens and treats with death. And what about poetry? Poetry is not up to tricks like this. Poetry is about reality and knows, or should, that dead *isn't*. Adam Zagajewski says, in 'Lecture on Mystery':

> We do not know what poetry is. We do not know what suffering is. We do not know what death is.
> We do know what mystery is.[14]

Poetry knows what dead is. As some part of us knows all that doesn't exist. All that we don't know. (And it should never, ever, score the cheap points of *death*. Why? Because the void questions death,[15] the void is the poem and we question the void. Ie, there's always life in it! It constitutes the circle and the idea of the 'is'.) As Jean Genet has so kindly pointed out to us: 'The author of a beautiful poem is always dead.'[16] He continues,

> The Mettray colonists [the prisoners] realized this, and we spoke of Harcamone, who had killed a nine-year-old girl, only in the past tense. Harcamone lived among us, but what circulated in the Colony was only his splendid envelope which had entered eternity. When we spoke to him, we never mentioned his crime, about which he must have known even less than we. What remained behind and moved about was a friend.[17]

There, the friend! This is what death is for us. What's left behind of the dead. It is who we can never know. The dead, on the other hand, like mystery, we know well. We understand nothing. We spend our lives asking questions for which we need no answer. And there are little answers so small that nobody wants them for any question: For law, the enormous, uncoverable distance between death and dead is closed by the idea of the lie in what is spoken. Law calls this the search for truth. For poetry, the measure of this same distance is pain and how pain, when translated, is joy.

And so our languages and discourses allow us to speak about 'being dead'. Utterance tries slopping life beyond death when death is simply in living and dead is there to absorb nothing. Tu Fu may have said 'Death certain as life, we advance'[18] but he surely knew that 'dead' is an adjective:

> Who can change it, who
> Stop it for even a single embrace – this dead
> Dazzling drunk in the wings of life we live?[19]

Law would call it disorderly. Poetry, the kindest kind of intoxication!

the present outcome of death

The judges were asked to determine the present outcome of death. This was a directive from the authorities who felt impelled to investigate because no-one had reported back. (From death, that is.) And a lack of information makes power nervous. Nervous power feels powerless. Seeks to find a purpose. What better than an inquiry and determination. *Holding court.*

Here's the lowdown:

1. The judges took no evidence. This despite the fact that death was beyond their experience.

2. Apropos of 1. (above), there were no witnesses.

2A. There is always one exception to the rule: 'the *actio*, a group of formulae designed to allow for the corporeal exteriorization of discourse: it dealt with a theater of expression, the actor-orator "expressing" his indignation, his compassion, etc.',[20] ie., a *ghost*.

'Let us talk about it as though it existed.'[21] Or so the judges intimated to each other. This intimacy became physical in a huddle of expensive scotch whiskey and half-remembered apparitions. Not that they didn't keep their wit about them, '[t]hough / it were the incarnation of dead grace'.[22])

3. There was also much laughter as is always the case when people become embarrassed by virtue of realizing they are 'participants' in something inevitable,

4. following things through to their natural conclusion. (That which *exceeds* a hangover. And if one would like to continue the humour, creates an excess, or waste. In other words, the corp(se) as 'too much person'.)

5. The judges produced a report that has not been made public.

6. It is rumoured that this 'judgment' – the reasoning of the judges – is to be treated as a precedent (*q.v.*) for any cases which follow which are determined to be of little or no importance.

What are we to make of this? The only clear conclusion that can be drawn is that all justices involved in the government report (The Present Outcome of Death), being of a goodly age already at the time of undertaking the commission, are now themselves undertaken (ie, dead). And despite their collective silence since, one might hope that their involvement with the report provided them with ample knowledge 'With which to interpret / The fresh decisions of death'.[23]

drifting with purpose
including an examination of how solace hides reality
& why the irresponsible and impure seek justification

Process. Collective process.

For example, the fiction that peace extends to the highways and ultimately to the whole realm. (Known as 'peace'.)

For example, all originating processes must be served personally. Service out of the jurisdiction can always be effected. There are no more high seas.

For example, outlaws are outlawed. Repeat. *Hors de la loi*. Brought in.

For example, 'A didactic purpose justifies itself in the mind of the teacher; a philosophical purpose justifies itself in the mind of the philosopher. It is not that one purpose is as justifiable as another but that some purposes are pure others impure.'[24]

Poetry's purpose is not – as law's is – to provide solatium.

Poetry's purpose is not – as law's is – to get there.

> Law is, after all, a social tool. It is only extrinsically important. Its actual value depends upon its success in promoting that which is intrinsically valuable.[25]

Poetry is neither extrinsically nor intrinsically important.

Poetry is not a tool.

Poetry is simply the tool's arc.

Its sweep.

The effort. Seeking. Going. Towards. Nothing in particular.

(What's real. The new reality.)

Poetry's purpose is unintended.

Poetry's purpose is undesigned.

Immaterial to the question and not to the point it is the *necessary act* —
neither useful nor useless function.

All that is undecided lives in poetry and aids decision.

Desiring rests in poetry and drifts.

Longing becomes unwilling.

> I who longed to be someone else, to weigh
> judgments, to read books, to hand down the law,
> will lie in the open out in these swamps;
> but a secret joy somehow swells my breast.
> I see at last I am face to face
> with my ... destiny.[26]

What is neither here or there.

But on the way.

Pure process.

Destiny's fate.

Disappearance.

The act of.

Use's other dimension.

How desire appears with no object.

ENDNOTES

1. Isabel Karpin.

2. Arundhati Roy, *The Algebra of Infinite Justice*, Flamingo, 2002, p264.

3. T.S. Eliot, 'Mr. Appollinax', *The Complete Poems and Plays*, Faber and Faber, London, 1969, p31: 'When Mr. Appollinax visited the United States / His laughter tinkled among the teacups. / … / He laughed like an irresponsible foetus. / His laughter was submarine and profound / Like the old man of the sea's / …'.

4. United States Supreme Court, abortion case where one of the judges drew an analagoy between the issues of the status of the foetus and the status of refugees (Haitian I think).

5. John M Conley and William M O'Barr, *Just Words: Law, Language and Power*, The University of Chicago Press, Chicago and London, 1998, p141: '[Brenda] Danet studied a Massachusetts trial in which a doctor who had performed an abortion was prosecuted for manslaughter. She analyzed the different ways in which prosecution and defense categorized the entity that had been aborted: "baby" and "little baby boy" by the prosecution, "fetus" and "products of procreation" by the defense.'

6. Mohandas K. Gandhi, http://www.sfheart.com/Gandhi.html.

7. *Ibid*.

8. Octavio Paz, 'Daybreak', *A Tale of Two Gardens: Poems from India, 1952-1995*, (Edited and Translated by Eliot Weinberger), New Directions, 1996, p50.

9. Valarie Mark, 'The Flip Side of Fetal Protection Policies: Compensating Children Injured Through Parental Exposure to Reproductive Hazards in the Workplace', *Golden Gate Law Review,* Vol. 22, 1992, p673 at p674.

10. Phillip Adams.

11. *Freeman v Frank* 10 Abb. Pr. [1860] 370 at 372.

12. See Dag Hammarskjold, *Markings,* (translated by W.H. Auden and Leif Sjoberg), Faber and Faber, London, 1964.

13. Giorgio Agamben, *Homo Sacer: Sovereign Power and Bare Life*, (translated by Daniel Heller-Roazen), Stanford University Press, Stanford, California, 1998, p27.

14. Adam Zagajewski, 'Lecture on Mystery', *Two Cities: On Exile, History and the Imagination,* (translated by Lillian Vallee), The University of Georgia Press, Athens, Georgia, 2002, p187.

15. Edmond Jabès, 'Journal III', *The Book of Questions, Volume II,* (translated by Rosmarie Waldrop), Wesleyan University Press, University Press of New England, Hanover, 1983, 1984, 1991, p259.

16. Jean Genet, *The Miracle of the Rose,* (translated by Bernard Frechtman), Penguin Books, London, 1951, 1965, p156.

17. *Ibid*.

18. *The Selected Poems of Tu Fu,* (translated by David Hinton), New Directions, New York,

1988, 1989, p12.

19. *Ibid*.

20. Roland Barthes, *The Pleasure of the Text,* (translated by Richard Miller), Hill and Wang, New York, 1975, p66.

21. *Ibid*.

22. Marianne Moore, 'To Statecraft Embalmed', *Complete Poems,* Macmillan Publishing Co., Inc., Penguin Books, 1981, p35.

23. Justo Jorge Padrón, 'The Secret of the Springs', *On the Cutting Edge,* (translated by Louis Bourne), Forest Books, London, Boston, 1988, p126.

24. Wallace Stevens, 'Adagia', from 'Aphorisms', *Opus Posthumous*, Revised, Enlarged and Corrected Edition, (Edited by Milton J Bates), Vintage Books, A Division of Random House, Inc., New York, 1990, p184. Stevens begins this paragraph with 'To give a sense of the freshness or vividness of life is a valid purpose for poetry.' and ends it with 'Seek those purposes that are purely the purpose of the pure poet.'

25. Ann Scales.

26. Jorge Luis Borges, 'Conjectural Poem', *Selected Poems 1923-1967*, (edited and with an Introduction and Notes by Norman Thomas di Giovanni), Allen Lane The Penguin Press, London, 1972, pp95 & 97.

ACKNOWLEDGEMENTS & NOTES

Parts of this book have appeared in *Alternative Law Journal*; *Green Integer Review* (USA); *Inklings*; *Mad Hatter's Review* (USA); *Stride* (UK); *Tattoo Highway* (USA).

'Caught on Film' was nominated for a Pushcart Prize, USA, 2006.

Epigraph from: Charles Baudelaire, 'Squibs (XXII)', *Intimate Journals* (translated by Christopher Isherwood), Panther Books, London, 1969, p44.